Sky Spy
Memoirs of a U-2 Pilot

Jim Carter

In loving memory of Sally,
Who inspired us all.

Acknowledgments

To those who made this idea a reality:
Pam Bronson, Dillon Carter, and especially
Debra Carter.

Contents:

PART I	PART II	PART III
Chapter 1	Chapter 1	Chapter 1
Chapter 2	Chapter 2	Chapter 2
Chapter 3	Chapter 3	Chapter 3
Chapter 4	Chapter 4	Chapter 4
Chapter 5	Chapter 5	Chapter 5
Chapter 6	Chapter 6	Chapter 6
Chapter 7	Chapter 7	Chapter 7
Chapter 8	Chapter 8	Chapter 8
Chapter 9	Chapter 9	Chapter 9
Chapter 10	Chapter 10	Chapter 10
Chapter 11		Chapter 11
Chapter 12		Chapter 12
Chapter 13		Chapter 13
Chapter 14		Chapter 14
Chapter 15		
Chapter 16		

Author's Note: The events in this book are true. Many of the names have been changed to protect their privacy or for national security reasons.

Preface

The frail, old priest bent down close to the bed-ridden woman. He tenderly caressed her forehead as he administered the last rites of the Catholic Church. He placed a small piece of the Eucharistic host in her mouth but she was unable to swallow it. I filled a cup with water from the bathroom sink and held my mother's head as she tried to sip the water.

My mother has advanced Alzheimer's disease and she has withered away to a mere shadow of her former self. Last month she fell and fractured her right hip. I studied her shrunken face as she lay in bed at the nursing home and my thoughts travelled back in time. This was the woman who had given me life and inspired my life. I was the last one she knew. Everyone else had faded from her mind. In time, she also forgot who I was. She hadn't spoken a meaningful word to me in three months and now she lay before me barely clinging to life. When the priest finished his blessing, I bent over my mom, Sally Carter, to stroke her hair and say goodbye. As I did so, she opened her eyes, looked into mine, and said "Thank You." Once again, my mother had amazed me. I shouldn't have been surprised; she had been amazing me my entire life.

I lived with my dad, mom, and three brothers in a row house in Philadelphia. I was 12 when my mom fled from my abusive, alcoholic father. One night, after a violent scene that included multiple cops and neighbors, my mom took my three younger brothers, Raymond, Randy, Greg and me to her parents' home in Wildwood, New Jersey. Their house was a safe haven for us. But simply being safe wasn't good enough for Sally. Jersey was very boring and the only people we knew there were my grandparents. She wanted nothing to do with my dad but all of our friends and relatives were in Philadelphia and she wanted to go back and find a new place for us. As soon as things stabilized and she was able to save some money, we moved back to Philadelphia. We couldn't afford a nice, middle-class neighborhood like the one we left. The only thing we could afford was a two-bedroom apartment at the back of a hardware store in the Germantown section of Philadelphia.

My mother worked two jobs in order to pay the bills. Her full-time job was a hostess in the local Howard Johnson's restaurant, and she had a part-time job as a supervisor in a Laundromat around the corner from our apartment. She took no public assistance and made a point of reminding us of that fact. She told us that life was difficult and if we ever wanted to improve our situation we had to work hard. She preached self-sufficiency and she practiced what she preached.

Since she was gone so much working, I became the male head of the house. I took care of my brothers. I got them up in the morning, made sure they dressed properly, served them breakfast, made their lunches, and got them off to school.

After school, we did homework, and then had dinner. An old standby that I made for my brothers countless times was a dinner of fish sticks and French fries; thank God for Mrs. Paul's.

Mom would come home exhausted from work, but she was never too tired to talk. She would tell me about her day at the restaurant and I would tell her about school or what my brothers had done that day.

The entrance to our apartment was through an alley, which led to a small, fenced-in yard of packed dirt. The door to the apartment opened to a small kitchen. Next to the kitchen was the living room, which had enough room for a small sofa and one single chair. The bedrooms were upstairs. My brothers and I shared one and Mom had the other. Our shared bathroom separated the bedrooms.

From our bedroom we could climb out on to a flat section of roof about ten feet square. Since we didn't have air conditioning, on stifling hot summer nights, we would climb on to the roof to cool off. The five of us would talk about our future. A common topic of conversation was how we were going to escape from this living hell we called our apartment. We also talked about our dreams and what we wanted to become. I had wanted to fly for as long as I could remember. Mom encouraged me to pursue my dream by stressing the importance of education. We lay on that roof looking up at the stars. The stars weren't that bright because of the light pollution from the city. Nevertheless, I could see them and wanted to reach them. From that roof behind the hardware store in Germantown, that seemed like an impossibility to me, but not to my mother. She assured me I could get there. If I worked hard and made the right choices, my dreams could come true. I just had to believe in and rely on myself. No one else was going to do it for me or give it to me. Encouraged by my Mom's example, I graduated from high school and then from St. Joseph's University in Philadelphia. I was lucky enough to be accepted into the Air Force ROTC program at St. Joseph's and I would be on my pathway towards becoming a pilot.

      Years later, when I achieved my dream, I vividly recalled those rooftop talks with Mom. Her work ethic had been passed on to me and made my dream a reality. This book tells the story of the journey to reach that dream.

PART I

Chapter 1

I attended St. Joseph's University in Philadelphia, Pennsylvania. My acceptance into the Reserve Officer Training Corp (ROTC) program at St. Joe's was my ticket into Air Force pilot training. I tested for the program as a sophomore and was one of four students chosen for the ROTC flight program. The ROTC program was a two-year program (junior and senior) and began with a six-week summer camp after my sophomore year. Our camp was held at Rickenbacker Air Force Base in Columbus Ohio. During these six weeks we learned all the basics of military life from marching to military courtesy. We also got a ride in a T-33 jet. It was truly a thrill for this 19 year old to go spinning through the sky in a real Air Force fighter plane. After the six-week course we knew how to march, knew all the ranks, both officer and enlisted, and we knew how make a proper military bed. But most important of all, I knew I loved to fly.

The ROTC pilot candidates were given a forty-hour course at the local airport flying a Cessna 150. The purpose of this course was to weed out those pilot candidates who may be best suited for other careers. This early screening process prevented sending an obviously weak candidate to pilot training only to have him wash out and then get re-assigned. The Cessna 150 we flew in the ROTC flight program was your basic single-engine, propeller driven, flight trainer. I soloed after about 10 hours of dual instruction. That feeling of accomplishment and freedom was unmatched in my life up to that time. We also went cross-country solo and got to see something other than the local traffic pattern. My first solo cross-country went from the Northeast Philadelphia airport to the Lancaster Pa. airport. After reaching Lancaster in good weather, I proceeded on the next leg of my great adventure to Cape May NJ airport. After landing and refueling in Cape May, I returned to my home base, PNE, Philadelphia Northeast airport. Every hour I spent in the air increased my confidence and stoked my excitement for the next phase of my career, USAF Pilot Training.

 I was commissioned as an officer and as expected, married my high school girlfriend, Doreen, after graduation. I was assigned to Laredo Air Force base. My new wife and I packed our stuff and headed for the Lone Star state

 It was 1969. The Air Force used the Cessna 172, the T-37 and the T-38 to instruct new students in the art of aviation. The Cessna 172 was almost identical to the Cessna 150 I flew in the ROTC program. It was just a little bigger and faster. The T-37 was the second jet I had ever experienced. The T-37 was a short, squatty, and loud aircraft with side-by-side seating. The T-38 was the advanced jet trainer and was configured with front and rear seating.

 Instructor pilots were assigned three or four students and they would normally fly with only those students. My T-37 IP was Captain Archie Morrell. Archie was about the most laid back man I'd ever met. I can't prove it but there were times during our flights when Ol' Archie took a quick nap. He would also pop his mask off occasionally and light up a Lucky Strike. Nothing ever fazed him. If things really got serious, he would always utter the same phrase, "Shit Oh Dear." That was apparently a favorite saying in Archie's hometown of Columbia, South Carolina.

My IP in the T-38 phase was Lt Steve Symon. Steve was a very intelligent guy from Massachusetts. His premature grey hair made him look older than his actual age of 27. My fellow students in the T-38 were Phil Duval and Randy Young. Phil was a big, likable guy from California and Randy was the epitome of the relaxed rebel from a small town in Mississippi. The four of us got along famously. Steve was the conductor and we were the orchestra. Phil, Randy and I helped each other through the program. We shared our mistakes and triumphs and before we knew it, the year had flown by and graduation was upon us.

By year's end, the group of 85 original pilots was narrowed by 33 percent. This was the average dropout rate and we survivors were feeling pretty good about ourselves as we lined up to receive our wings.

I had a double celebration that month. Not only did I earn my wings, but just before graduation, my daughter, Krista, was born.

Assignments for bases were awarded just prior to graduation. Our class assignments ran the gamut from the F-4 fighter to the B-52 bomber. I was assigned to fly the C-130 at Pope Air Force Base in Fayetteville, North Carolina. But before heading to our assignments we had to learn to fly our assigned planes. All C-130 training was held at Little Rock Air Force Base, Arkansas. I was excited to head to another southern state for six weeks of intensive training.

Chapter 2

In the early 1970's the C-130 was the workhorse of worldwide airlift. Often referred to as The Hercules, the C-130 was first built in the early 1950's with the "A" model. Over 40 models of the aircraft are in service today in over 60 nations. The current model is the "J". I flew the "E" model.

Over the years, small improvements were made to the C-130. The engines were beefed up, another blade was added to the three-bladed prop, instrumentation was improved and the landing gear was strengthened to support heavy loads. The airplane was built like a tank. Four turboprop engines and multiple redundancies for safety, the C-130 was capable of landing just about anywhere, including dirt strips only 3,000 feet long. The Hercules earned its nickname by being a strong, tough, dependable airplane.

As a pilot, there's a certain comfort knowing that your aircraft can continue to fly with one or even two engines shut down. The C-130 was used for every conceivable mission from troop dropping to trash hauling – the pilot's term for cargo delivery.

All pilots, both aircraft commanders and copilots are trained to the same flying standards. The aircraft commander bore the ultimate responsibility for the entire crew and aircraft. The copilot's job was to act as second-in-command and share the flying duties with the aircraft commander.

It was quite a switch to transition from the two-engine T-38 trainer used in pilot training, to the four-engine C-130. The T-38 was a twin seat, twin engine, fighter-type trainer. In the T-38, pilots either flew solo or with an instructor. We only had to listen to the instructor on the intercom and air traffic control on the radio.

The C-130 was much slower than the T-38 but a whole lot busier. The C-130 co-pilot is part of a five-man crew and has to communicate with the other four on the intercom and listen to air traffic control on the radio.

A typical 4-hour training mission consisted of takeoffs, landings, emergency procedures, and instrument approaches. In addition, new pilots learned to coordinate efforts with the rest of the crew.

After finishing the six-week course in Little Rock, I was transferred to Pope Air Force Base to report to the 779th Tactical Airlift Squadron. Pope would be a new beginning for us. Doreen and I had both been born and raised in Philadelphia and had not had an opportunity for traveling much other than going to the Jersey shore. One of the reasons I chose the C-130 assignment was because of its mission: worldwide tactical airlift. To a 22-year-old kid right out of flight training, the "worldwide" part was very appealing. Our flight instructors at Little Rock had been in the C-130 for several years and had been around the world a few times. Their stories only fueled our desire to experience what the future held for us.

Chapter 3

Doreen, Krista and I moved to North Carolina the September of 1970. Pope Air Force base is where I would be stationed for at least the next three years. As an officer with a family I qualified for officer housing on base. But there was no officer housing available on this busy Air Force base. Instead they offered us housing at adjacent Fort Bragg. Fort Bragg housing was not very impressive but the only other option was to rent something off base. Without much money saved up our choice was clear. We chose a home at Fort Bragg.

As we drove into the neighborhood and located our new home, we noticed a housing unit about 300 yards down the street marked with crime scene tape. It was being patrolled by several Military Police (MPs). It turned out to be the home of Dr. Jeffrey McDonald whose family had been found murdered. Dr. McDonald claimed "crazed hippies" had killed his family. Being that Fort Bragg was an open base, there was fear that a group of crazy hippies could come into the base and murder other unsuspecting families. Home security for my family became a high priority and I decided to look for off base housing as soon as I could afford it.

The first pilot I met in my squadron at Pope was Irv Ashton. Irv lived just two houses down from Doreen and I in Fort Bragg. He came over and introduced himself as we were moving in. Irv seemed like a nice guy. My first impression of Irv was that he was regular and easygoing. I would learn in the months to come that Irv was one crazy motherfucker.

Irv was very friendly and he invited us to his home to meet his wife, Cynthia. We showed up at his door with a bottle of wine, which he placed atop his fully stocked bar. Our bottle was merely a drop in the bucket among all the other booze Irv possessed. It turned out that Irv loved to drink. I'm no teetotaler but Irv made me look like a man doing an impression of John Calvin. I didn't even try to keep up with him.

Irv had a state of the art quadrophonic stereo system. He picked up the system on his last temporary duty (TDY) to Taiwan. It was a beautiful, top of the line system, but all he had to play on it were old, scratched up 45s from his college days at the Citadel. He picked out "Louie Louie" by the Kingsmen and threw it on the turntable. The resulting noise from this four-speaker nightmare prompted calls from angry neighbors. Irv listened to their complaints and promptly took care of the complaining neighbors by cranking up the volume. A visit from the MPs however, convinced him to turn it off.

Like most new squadron couples, he and Cynthia furnished their home from college leftovers and yard sale specials. Their dining room set was a folding card table with matching chairs. It was simple but cozy. We ate dinner seated on the folding chairs.

During dinner I felt a hand on my thigh. I glanced at Doreen and both her hands were visible. I looked over at Cynthia and she flashed a seductive smile as her hand went higher. About the same time I saw Doreen jump as Irv's hand disappeared below the table. Her reaction was more vocal than mine; she shrieked and stood up. Not wanting to be left behind, I popped up also. We grabbed our things and fled the scene. Later I learned that this was the standard "dinner at Irv's." His theory was: "If you ask everyone, one or two are bound to say yes."

At Pope I continued training on the C-130. There was constant training on the basics plus some advanced items like formation flying, airdrops, short field takeoffs and landings and exotic maneuvers like "LAPES" drops.

LAPES stands for Low Altitude Parachute Extraction System. The idea behind LAPES is to have a C-130 come roaring across the ground at 150 knots, 10 feet off the ground, or deck as we call it, with the cargo ramp lowered. On a given signal, the loadmaster would release a parachute that connected to a pallet containing cargo of anything from Frosted Flakes to field artillery. When the chute inflates, it drags the pallet out of the airplane and, if all goes well, the pallet flops gently to the ground and skids to a halt. This system was developed and tested by one of the greatest C-130 pilots ever to don the flight suit, Lieutenant Colonel Benny Fioritto. (Years later, Benny would become my squadron commander.)

From a pilot's perspective, the LAPES drop was an exercise in control. The airplane had to be right on airspeed and altitude for the load to exit the aircraft and hit the ground at the correct angle. Too much nose up or down at the moment of extraction meant that the load would likely tumble, sending rice or howitzers every which way. Depending on how heavy the pallet of cargo was, the flight controls of the C-130 would change violently during the maneuver. This was caused by the shifting weight on the aircraft's center of gravity (CG). This caused the airplane to pitch up and down and the pilot had to keep it level.

All aircraft, from the Cessna 150 to the Airbus 380, must be loaded to keep the CG within acceptable limits. Everything must be taken into consideration: the empty weight of the airplane, the crew weight, the fuel, and the load carried.

On a tactical exercise at Nellis AFB Nevada, I sat in the observation stands as a Pope C-130 attempted a LAPES drop of a Jeep. As the aircraft roared by, the chute came out and then abruptly stopped in mid-air. As the Jeep was sliding out, the pallet jammed in the rollers and got stuck sideways in the door. This is one of the worst nightmares for a C-130 driver. Ten feet off the ground, full aft CG with an inflated chute trailing behind and dragging you down. Quick action by the loadmaster to detach the chute saved the day. The crew was able to climb the airplane back up in spite of the aft CG. The Jeep was jammed in the door and not moving but they were able to land safely and had a good war story for the bar that night.

Parachute drops were an important part of our mission. While at Pope, we regularly trained with the 82nd Airborne Division. The normal airdrop mission usually consisted of three or more aircraft flying in formation over a specified route leading to one of the Ft. Bragg drop zones (DZs). These DZs are close to Pope, with the largest being Sicily DZ. Other DZs at Bragg include, Salerno, St Mere Eglise, Holland, All American, and Nijmegen. They were named for the DZs used during D-Day in World War II.

We usually dropped 30 to 50 troops from 1500 to 2000 feet. The navigator kept us on course throughout. The navigator would call, "green light" to signal when the troops were ready to drop. The troops exited through both side rear doors. These were standard static line jumps. A thick metal wire ran from front to back about six feet off the deck on both sides of the aircraft. The troops would hook their chutes on to the line when it was getting close to jump time. At "green light" they started jumping out the doors. As they exited, their leader line, hooked to the plane's static line, would pull the chute out of its pack causing it to inflate - most of the time. If the main didn't open they inflated a spare chute worn on their chest.

Initially, these jumps were exciting for me. Watching these kids jump out of a perfectly good airplane was fascinating. The novelty of the exercise wore off after a while and it just became another mission. Flying these repetitive missions became boring.

Then came working with the Green Berets and things were not so dull anymore. The Green Berets were the elite at Fort Bragg. They were highly skilled, intelligent and fearless. They did things like HALO drops. HALO stood for High Altitude Low Opening parachute drops. We would drop these guys out at 15,000 feet and they would free-fall down to 1000 feet before opening their chute; like I said, fearless.

Even more amazing were their night drops. A Green Beret would be situated on the ground and mark the drop zone for his airborne teammates. We would fly to the pre-determined coordinates and their on-board spotter would stick his head out the door looking for the DZ, many times marked by the spotter on the ground with just a flashlight. When the on-board Green Beret saw the DZ he would calculate his release point, call "green light," and the guys would jump out into the blackness. The Green Beret training missions were the tactical side of the airlift business. There was also a humanitarian aspect to our work and I would become very familiar with this in the coming months.

When I finished my training at Pope, I was termed "combat ready" meaning I was ready to go anywhere the Air Force needed me. The C-130 was in high demand around the world so I wouldn't have to wait long.

Chapter 4

The first opportunity to travel came in 1971 during the Bangladesh independence movement on a mission called Operation Bonny Jack.

In 1947, British India was divided into the independent countries of India and Pakistan. The two countries have been involved in four wars since then. The dispute over Kashmir has been the cause of three of these wars. In 1971 the two went to war over the attempted secession of East Pakistan from West Pakistan. The crisis was created by the political battle between Sheik Mujib, leader of East Pakistan and Yahya Bhutto of West Pakistan. The east declared their independence and this caused the Pakistani Army to crack down on the millions of Bengalis living in the east. A nine-month war of independence began in March of 1971. There were reports of mass slaughter and rape of civilians. People were fleeing the genocide and the US Air Force was asked to go in there and help.

Both the US and the USSR had vital interests at stake. The Russians backed the Indian government; our government backed the Pakistanis. Each superpower picked a side and kept them supplied with planes and munitions in order to maintain the balance of power. Neither of the superpowers wanted to get involved in a shooting war so the only way to intervene was through humanitarian aid. This meant that both would send airlift support to help with the humanitarian crisis. Airlift to the rescue.

The request for airlift had arrived and we were tasked with supplying three aircraft and six crews for a two-month deployment to India. I was eager to travel and immediately volunteered.

Operation Bonny Jack called for C-130 crews to travel between India and Pakistan. From a base in India we were to fly into East Pakistan (soon to be Bangladesh) and deliver food and medical supplies. On the return trip, we would load up with refugees and fly them back to India where they would be assigned to resettlement camps.

The crew assignments were published, and ours was as follows: Aircraft Commander, Captain Herb Gaston; Navigator, Captain Bill Corcoran; Flight Engineer MSgt Ed Parman; Loadmaster SSgt Cliff Brown and yours truly, 1st Lt Jim Carter, co-pilot. There would be three airplanes flying with two crews each. The crews would switch off for each leg of the flight.

Herb was a Tennessee native who attended Vanderbilt University. He took pre-med in college and planned to become a doctor until he discovered flying and all that changed. After college he went to Air Force Officer Candidate School and then on to pilot training. He had been in the C-130 for about five years.

Our navigator, Bill Corcoran, also wanted to be a pilot but he washed out of pilot training and became a navigator. Bill was the crew clown always coming up with the funniest jokes and raunchiest stories.

Ed Parman was a career enlisted man who had been in the Air Force for 22 years when I first met him. Ed knew the airplane inside out and was a wealth of information about its systems and limitations.

Cliff Brown was the loadmaster and the youngest member of the crew. He had been on the 130 his entire career and had delivered everything from horseshoes to hand grenades.

We departed Pope just after sundown heading up the US coastline to eastern Long Island before heading out to sea. The first stop on the way to India would be Lajes Field in the Azores, a mid Atlantic pit stop for aircraft heading to and from Europe. The Azores, a Portuguese possession, are a series of rocks in the middle of the ocean and Lajes is an airbase on the island of Terceira.

It was a clear, moonless night with the stars spread across the sky in a dazzling array. We settled in at our cruising altitude of 25,000 feet and rolled on through the endless blackness.

Occasionally, we could see lights in the ocean and the conversation turned to discussing those poor bastards manning those lonely ships in the deep darkness below us. Navigator Bill Corcoran loved to communicate with the ocean stations whenever he crossed the Atlantic. These ocean stations were ships anchored at specific spots. Their job was to relay weather information used in forecasting. They would report their observations via radio, on both VHF (Very High

Frequency) and HF (High Frequency) bands. They also aided in search and rescue operations and acted as relays when needed for trans Atlantic flights. The standard tour of duty on these ships was three to four weeks; so you can imagine how eager these guys were to speak to any aircrew transiting the Atlantic.

Bill was the only navigator I ever knew who talked to the ships, and he loved it as much as they did. After talking the latest gossip, news, or sports, the subject turned to jokes - the cruder the better - and limericks. Bill would throw out a joke or a limerick and they would try to come back with a topper.

Bill exchanged several limericks with Ocean Station Echo that night. They asked us where we were headed and Bill said: "the Azores." So they came back with the following:

"There once was a girl from the Azores,
whose body was covered with sores,
and the dogs in the street
would chew on the green meat
that hung in festoons from her drawers."

Not to be outdone, Bill shot back:

"There was a young man from Poole,
who found a red ring round his tool.
He went to the clinic
where the doctor, a cynic,
said, "wash it, 'tis lipstick you fool."

So they responded:

"There once was a hermit named Dave
who kept a dead whore in his cave.
She was missing one tit
and smelled like shit.
But think of the money he saved."

Nothing is quite as monotonous as an ocean crossing at night but these exchanges kept us awake and laughing like hell. The exchanges went back and forth while we were in radio range, usually a half-hour. Before we lost contact, we promised to catch them on the way back.

These ocean stations were gradually phased out, replaced by weather buoys. The last ship was retired in 1977. The weather buoys were cheaper but not nearly as funny.

We arrived in the Azores on June 2, 1971 after a 9-hour flight. The chain of islands known collectively as the Azores is famous for its bread and wine and we heavily sampled both. It's a quiet, beautiful place. At least it was until we arrived.

Since we were only at the base for one night we were restricted and told to remain on base. This meant nothing to Irv Ashton who was the co-pilot on another crew headed to India. While the rest of us joined up at the Officers Club for some carousing, Irv decided to head into town. His goal, always the same regardless of location, was to drink prodigious amounts of alcohol and have sex with any female that had a pulse.

Unfortunately for Irv, he picked the Mayor's daughter. The Mayor himself interrupted him mid - act. Irv managed to gather most of his clothing before fleeing out of the daughter's window. He got back on the base by climbing a security fence but snagged his pants on the barbed wire. He showed up back at the Bachelor Officers Quarters sans pants but still alive.

We left the Azores hung-over but happy to be moving again to the next stop on the road to India, Madrid, Spain.

Lucky for us, our aircraft needed some minor maintenance work so we had two days to see the sights in Madrid. That meant trying to cram in as much as possible without benefit of sleep. It was tough, but we succeeded. Our tourist whirlwind included the Prado Museum, Flamenco dancers, and tapas bars. We all thoroughly enjoyed ourselves, and this time Irv behaved. My favorite parts were the amazing artwork at the Prado and the intricate steps of the Flamenco dancers.

The weather was beautiful as we made our way to the next stop on our journey, Aviano Air Base, near Pisa, Italy. Seeing the Alps for the first time was breathtaking. On a sunny day, we flew into Italy at 22,000 feet, or about 7,000 feet over the jagged peaks of the Alps. We marveled at the beautiful, intricate villages that dotted the valleys between the peaks. I envied their beautiful countryside and their splendid isolation.

Once again, a two-day break allowed us to "go local" and sample the dining and shopping. Among the specialties of the Pisa area were beautiful handcrafted globes they sold in the artisanal shops that lined the streets. The globes were large, old-world style, about 2 feet in diameter and suspended in a beautiful wooden gimbal. Best of all, the globes opened at the equator to reveal a bar inside. Those that could afford one loaded it on the airplane and off we went.

One of the advantages of the C-130 is that you can shop for souvenirs from your travels and store it all on the plane as you move around the world. We packed bread and wine from the Azores, guitars from Madrid, and globe bars from Italy. The airplanes were filling up and we hadn't even reached our destination yet.

Our next stop was Dhahran, Saudi Arabia. We arrived at night, the stars were twinkling and the outside air temperature was 106 degrees F. It was a dry heat and there was a fine coating of sand on everything. The people we encountered were not very friendly. If I had to live in those conditions, I'd be pissed too!

The only memorable nugget I can relay from this stop was my encounter with a Saudi commode. They don't have toilets like ours but instead have a hole in the floor with a ceramic footpad on either side. I couldn't understand why if they could manufacture ceramic footpads they couldn't make a toilet. Middle East tradition I guess.

Just before we left, I had to use the facilities. It was dark and all the stalls were unlit. I unzipped my flight suit and proceeded to take care of business. The flight suit is a one-piece garment made of a fireproof material called Nomex. To don it, you step into it, pull it up, stick your arms in the sleeves, and zip. It zips from the crotch to the neck and has zippered compartments on the chest, legs and arms to hold all the crap the typical pilot carried around with him: Hat (in the leg pocket when not on the head), sunglasses, pens, cigarettes, logbook, survival knife, small flashlight, keys, and wallet. It was just like a ladies purse only worn as a garment that kept you from burning alive in a post crash fire. It was not the most comfortable thing to deal with while squatting over a shit-stained hole in the ground.

So there I was, balancing myself on ceramic footpads, in a full squat, while trying to hit the target hole in the dark. I couldn't even estimate the last time this place had been cleaned. The stink was like a living organism. I only managed to survive it by mouth-breathing. This was not for the faint of heart, but when nature calls .....

When I finished, I availed myself of some of the industrial strength sandpaper that they used for toilet paper and cleaned up as best as I could. My one concern during this process was keeping my flight suit out of the line of fire. I zipped up and made my way to the aircraft for the next leg of the trip.

Once airborne, we all noticed a strong, foul odor, like a St. Bernard had taken a dump in the cockpit after eating some bad Indian food. All non-essential activity stopped until we could locate the source of this rank obscenity.

After an hour of searching, the source of the smell was found. It was under the collar of my flight suit. It seems one of the previous users of my stall didn't have the same accuracy as I did, and my collar had picked up a brown souvenir from our stop at Dhahran. I set some kind of record unstrapping from my seat and peeling off the flight suit. I actually thought about throwing it away rather than washing it, but since I only had four of them, I kept it. I wrapped it up in a plastic bag and stuffed the fowl package into my suitcase.

The next day we arrived in India. Our destination was an Indian airbase in Gauhati, in the state of Assam in northeast India. Assam sits just southeast of Bhutan and our view of the Himalayas was spectacular. Earlier in the trip I had been very impressed with the Alps. The Himalayas, however, were the major leagues of mountain ranges. They were massive in both height and width. These mountains were at least twice as tall as the Alps and the chain seemed to stretch to infinity. Even though we didn't have to fly over them they were nonetheless awe-inspiring.

In stark contrast to the mountains was the jungle. Gauhati sits along the Brahmaputra River with jungle bordering the other side of town.

After landing, we secured the aircraft and met representatives of the Indian Army and Air Force. These gentlemen would be our guides helping us acclimate to life in India. Since the British Raj ruled India for so many years, these officers mirrored their British counterparts, from the handlebar moustaches to the uniforms. The first order of business was a tour of our quarters.

This is where we would be living for the next six weeks. The officers would be in one building, the enlisted men in another. The buildings were not modeled on the Taj Mahal. They were originally meant as barracks for the Indian Army, whose standards were nowhere near the ones for the US Army, much less, our Air Force. These were cinder block buildings. Each room had built-in shelving on the walls, and a single bed, equipped with a mosquito net. The communal bathrooms had the same ceramic footpad arrangement as the ones in Dhahran, but at least now I had some practice. The communal showers came with an unlimited supply of cold water. There were hot and cold faucets but they both yielded only cold water.

The windows of our barracks were covered with chicken wire. When we asked our Indian government representative about it he assured us it was meant to keep out bugs. It turned out he wasn't kidding.

Once we settled into our new home, we attended our newcomer briefing. The Indian officers talked about the weather conditions we would be dealing with in the Gauhati area. The word "thunderstorm" was use quite frequently. High heat and humidity also figured prominently in the briefing; so we had that going for us.

The discussion then turned to the local wildlife. We were warned not to go out alone because there were tigers roaming through the jungle and they would occasionally come into the outskirts of town and carry off the unlucky villager. Snakes, particularly cobras, were part of the landscape, along with various and sundry bugs. I don't ever recall the subject of man-eating tigers coming up while I spent twelve months in pilot training. Live and learn.

We were also instructed on how to deal with the cows. Cows were sacred in India and they had free reign over everything. Cows had the right of way every time. If a cow felt like lying down in the middle of the street, which they often did, the traffic would have to go around them. We were not allowed to impede them in any way. We were also warned to steer clear of the hashish vendors who prominently displayed their goods on many street corners in town.

We went to India to fly and boy did we. We flew every day, with an occasional, very rare, day off. Our day started early and went on until dark. Luckily, we were young, eager pilots looking to build flying time and experience. India provided both of those.

The airplanes were loaded in Gauhati with pallets of rice. Our pallets were flat, rectangular metal transport structures with locks on the side. The rice was loaded on the pallets and secured with a tie-down strap. The pallets would slide into the airplane on a built in roller system on the floor and then lock into position. This roller system made loading and unloading a snap. A guy on a forklift and a loadmaster on the plane could finish the job in 15 minutes. After loading up we flew across the border into East Pakistan. We landed at a forward operating base and offloaded the rice. The rice was removed from the pallets and then the empty pallets were placed back on the aircraft.

Now came the fun part.

On our return trip we loaded up with refugees who had assembled at this operating base hoping they could make it to India. The problem was that there were only the flat pallets for them to sit on; and there was no shortage of refugees. These people had been driven from their homes. The majority of them were Hindus fleeing the wrath of the East Pakistani Muslim Army. India was the only safe haven they could hope to reach. They fled with only what they could carry, and some had been on the road for weeks. There were thousands who wished to go. International aid workers picked the lucky passengers who would go with us.

The refugees streamed into a temporary camp, which had been set up near the airfield. They were given the basics of food and shelter until it was their turn to be transported to more permanent camps in West Bengal. International aid workers from the UN interviewed the refugees and established their priority for evacuation. Our job was to take them safely to the refugee camp in West Bengal. Of course the term "safely" encompasses many items when discussing airplanes, especially those operating in remote areas of India.

Just as with the LAPES (low altitude parachute extraction system) drops the loadmaster had to worry about getting the center of gravity just right, which could be somewhat tricky to do with dozens of refugees filling the airplane. All had to be calculated by the loadmaster to ensure that our center of gravity was "in the green." To seat all these people, the loadmasters had to be creative. We were working with the flat metal floor of the pallets, and we wanted to carry as many refugees as possible. But these were small people; there were no overweight refugees.

We were able to jam many in the plane and still stay within our CG limits. The loadmaster would start at the front of the cargo compartment and sit them in a straight line across the pallet, facing forward. As soon as one line was seated, he started in on the next and so on until we reached the maximum number that could be carried on that particular flight. The loadmaster would take a cargo strap and run it across the passengers' laps and secure it on the other side. Voila! Instant all coach accommodations.

The C-130 could hold five pallets. Figuring ten people across, we could fit 50 people per pallet. At a maximum, we could fit 250 refugees if all the CG numbers worked out. We never got that many on a flight. Our record was 218 on a mission flown by Operations Officer, Lt Col "Sweats" Tollefson.

Sweats earned his nickname by sweating constantly and always sweating the small stuff.

Whenever I saw Sweats he was red-faced and smoking a cigarette. I don't think he ever slept or had his blood pressure drop below 170/100. He was a chain smoking worrywart who was scared to death of letting people do the jobs they were trained to do. "Sweats" was not a delegator. He was a doer and a re-checker. If it were possible, Sweats would have flown all the missions himself while simultaneously manning the command post and sweeping the flight line with a broom stuck up his ass.

Although it was rewarding for us to help so many people survive, we did have challenges to work through.

The flying facilities were primitive or nonexistent. We were used to accurate navigation facilities so we could get from point A to point B in the weather. These facilities didn't exist in India in 1971. The flying was VFR or "visual flight rules." The navigators needed to see the ground in order to get us to our destination. If the weather rolled in, we didn't fly. Many of the airfields were dirt strips. We parked the airplanes on the grass, which had been overlaid with perforated steel planking (PSP). PSP was reinforced steel planks with holes. These planks were laid on the ground to prevent the aircraft from sinking into the grass or mud. It is still used at remote airfields around the globe.

And then there was the one factor none of us had counted on, the smell. Nothing in my life had prepared me for this smell. Most of these refugees had been on the road, fleeing death and destruction. There were no showers or baths on the refugee trail. They fled with only the clothes on their backs, and they were still wearing them. They ate large amounts of curry and spices, all of which came out in their sweat and breath. It was a sharp, acrid, painful, nearly nauseating odor that the stifling heat did nothing to alleviate. It was June in India and the temperature and humidity stayed in the nineties. It was tolerable in the open air but closed up on an airplane with 200 of them for an hour-long flight –Stink City.

When I first experienced it I had trouble breathing. I had to put on my oxygen mask. This gave a new and terrible meaning to the term "eye watering."

After a few days of this routine we were able to somewhat tolerate the smell; but it still watered the eyes. We dropped the refugees off at resettlement camps where they would later move on to more permanent housing. Even living in these tent cities was a vast improvement to what their lives had been like those last few months. Doctors, aid-workers, and UN personnel, all helped out at the camps.

The end of our long flying day meant a shower, a fresh set of clothes, a bite to eat and later, a gathering at the "Officers Club" for a few beers and war stories. Since space was so restricted we had combined the Officers and NCOs clubs into one. It was a 10-foot by 20-foot cinderblock room with bench seats and Indian beer. I had never tried Indian beer before, but quickly became a convert. It had two distinct advantages over American beer: first, it came in liter bottles, and second, it was 8 to 10% alcohol. The taste was richer and more biting than American beer. Those of us who had grown up on 3.2 beer were soon stumbling around walking into walls and trying to speak Hindi to our Indian Air Force buds; it was pretty good stuff.

After the first night at the club, and a few beers in, I made my way back to my room. I had only been asleep for a few minutes when my fellow co pilot and neighbor called me into his room.

"What's up Vince?" I asked through my beery, sleepy haze.

"Tell me what the fuck this is," he said pointing to his chicken-wire screen. Something was caught in the wire and it was still alive. It looked like some kind of prehistoric bug. Not being an entomologist, I squashed it with my flashlight and went back to bed, dreaming of prehistoric bugs.

The next day I corralled our Indian Army rep and showed him the remains from the previous night.

"Oh, that's a rice bug," he said.

"Are you shitting me, that's a bug?" I exclaimed.

"Oh yes sir, very good eating you know," he replied.

I had no response. The whole concept of a six-inch long bug flying around had eluded me up to now. And as for eating it, as my buddy Vinnie would say, "Fuggettaboutit."

So as it turned out, our guide on that first day in India had been correct. The chicken wire kept the bugs out, at least the bigger ones. The rice bugs weren't the only natives we had to get used to. One night I was awakened from a sound sleep by the sound of something scratching across the concrete floor. I turned on the light and discovered a half dozen crabs walking in a straight line across my floor. These crabs were about six inches across and they marched with military precision. I didn't know whether to smash them or cook them. Instead I let them go on their way. I didn't know where they had come from or where they were going so I just turned out the light and went back to sleep. I never saw the crabs again after that night.

Chapter 5

About three weeks into our mission we took a trip to New Delhi. Each flight crew was given one weekend of R&R there. We stayed in a nice hotel called the Oberoi Intercontinental. There we could take unlimited warm showers and experience the joys of air conditioning. We would start the day with a big breakfast in the hotel's opulent dining room. Real eggs and fresh juice were not available in Gauhati so we made sure we got to get our fill of these luxuries while in New Delhi.

After our big breakfast, we would wander the streets taking in the sights and sounds of this very crowded city. One of my favorite activities was souvenir hunting. There were countless side streets with shops selling everything from spittoons to sitars. I mention sitars because I bought one. I had no musical background but Ravi Shankar and George Harrison played the sitar so how hard could it be, right? My backup plan was to use it as a display piece just in case my playing didn't work out.

My lasting impression of New Delhi was the crowds. So many people packed into small spaces. We westerners were used to so much more room. Even the buses and trains were jammed to overflowing. I was standing on a street corner in Delhi and watched a bus approach the intersection. The bus was packed full and there were people hanging off both sides. I held my breath because I felt sure that the bus would roll over. The hangers-on knew what was coming, and as the bus started to lean precariously into the turn they leaped off. The bus righted itself and then they all jumped back on. Only in India.

I was proud of my new sitar and showed it around the base when I returned to Gauhati. I tried unsuccessfully to play it at the Club that night. Maybe the Indian beer had something to do with my ineptitude. At least I managed to learn how to hold it before we left India. But the sitar was destined to decorate my living room.

My flight engineer, Ed, was at the club that night. Ed was a very good engineer but he was very fond of the "sauce." He fell in love with the Indian beer and had more than his share that night. When he started speaking in tongues we convinced him to turn in. His building was only about 20 yards from the club so we sent him on his way, confident that he could find his way home.

Around 2 a.m. we called it a night and headed back to our rooms. An irrigation ditch ran along the path between the buildings. It was about three feet wide and three feet deep. As I walked along the path I glanced down into the ditch and thought I saw something. It looked like a body, but I couldn't be sure. I shined my light on it and discovered a body covered with something. And that something was moving. On closer inspection, I could see it was Ed, sleeping peacefully, and covered with rice bugs! Yuck. I yelled for some help and three or four of us yanked him out of the ditch and brushed the rice bugs off. He was none the worse for wear and was ready to head back to the club. We convinced him the club was closed and walked him to his room

Our crew did get to make one additional side trip while in Gauhati. We were tasked with delivering several pallets of medicine to Calcutta. Our destination was the Calcutta International Airport and all went smoothly, arriving right on schedule in beautiful weather. They parked us on a military ramp right next to a Russian airplane, an AN-12. Before I describe the plane, just a brief explanation of the Russian philosophy of aircraft design: copy the Americans but try to make it bigger and faster. We were scoping out their aircraft from afar when we saw the Russian pilots disembark and walk towards our C-130. Keep in mind that in 1971 we were cold war enemies. We looked at these Russians with a mixture of caution and excitement. None of us had ever met a Russian pilot and none of us spoke Russian. They came up to us smiling, excited and spoke broken but understandable English. Basically, they were in awe of our airplane, our technology, and us. They wanted to show us their aircraft and hoped we would reciprocate. Sounded good to us, so off we went into the AN-12.

The AN-12 was a Russian attempt to copy the C-130. The exterior of the Russian plane did look like the C-130, but inside was another story. In the cockpit, the two pilots sat up high with the throttle quadrant between them. Below the pilots was a flat bench where the navigator would lay face down looking through the glass observation bubble. Next to the navigator's station were his navigation aids, Esso road maps.

The AN-12 did not have hydraulics and it cruised at 300+ knots, so it took some strength to operate the flight controls. This probably explained why both pilots looked like weight lifters. Both pilots would operate the controls simultaneously. The navigator would give them a countdown, then say "turn right" or "turn left" and both pilots would execute together.

The cockpit instrumentation was right off the set of "Young Frankenstein." Tubes, rolling drums, exposed wires, giant levers, etcetera, were everywhere. The back of the airplane was even more startling than the cockpit. In the C-130, we had our roller system to easily load and unload freight. No such system existed in the AN-12. It had a plain floor with park benches screwed to the wall. They told us that any airborne equipment drop was an emergency procedure only.

When we showed them the 130 they were mesmerized. Even our old (to us) instrumentation was light years ahead of theirs. A look at our roller system in the back had them yammering to each other accompanied by non-stop pointing and gesturing.

But those Commies could bargain. We had some items they wanted and they had genuine Russian hooch. We swapped several bottles of their vodka for our blue jeans and Marlboros. When we left Calcutta, we were a little wiser in international relations, and a few bottles of Russian vodka richer.

We spent six weeks in India and as bad as conditions were, they were the fastest six weeks of my life.

We completed our mission to India in the summer of 1971. Hostilities against the Bangladeshi separatists continued through the fall.

On December 3, 1971, Pakistan launched pre-emptive air strikes on 11 Indian airbases. This caused India to declare war on Pakistan and to enter the conflict on the side of the separatists. The resulting India-Pakistan War lasted 13 days, one of the shortest wars in history. During these 13 days, Indian and Pakistani forces clashed on both the eastern and western fronts. The war came to an abrupt end after the Eastern Command of the Pakistani Armed Forces signed the instrument of surrender on December 16, 1971. This marked the birth of the new nation of Bangladesh.

The statistics of this struggle for independence are shocking. Between 90,000 and 93,000 members of the Pakistani Armed Forces were taken as prisoners of war by the Indian Army. As many as three million civilians were killed in this conflict. It is estimated that the Pakistani Armed Forces raped up to 400,000 Bengali women. Eight to ten million people fled the country seeking refuge in India.

Our mission to India saved thousands of lives but we all felt unsatisfied, not because of those we helped, but for those we could not.

Chapter 6

When it came time to leave India the hot topic of discussion was: which way do we go? Back west the way we came, or continue east and make a complete circuit of the globe. Naturally, all us young guys wanted to go east just to see the places we hadn't been. We finally won out and headed east to the states.

After careful planning, the navigators came up with an itinerary for our return. The first stop would be U-Tapao Air Base Thailand, then Yakota Air Base, Japan, Elmendorf AFB, Alaska and finally Pope.

Before leaving India, we had to complete the one mission that every red-blooded American pilot was compelled to do: shop for souvenirs. In addition to the stuff we had already picked up in Spain and Italy we added Indian room screens. These were beautiful mahogany, tri-fold room divider screens, inlaid with brass on one side and ivory on the other. This was definitely a must have item for every C-130 pilot's home. Plus, it went nicely with the sitar - which I now knew how to hold. Space was getting tight on our airplanes: globe bars, guitars, sitars, room screens, silks, paintings and carvings all had to go somewhere. After the souvenirs were loaded, off we went to Thailand.

U-Tapao Air Base, Thailand, about 90 miles southeast of Bangkok, was beautifully situated on the Gulf of Siam and the first stop on the road home. We had been away from home for over six weeks and we were all eager to get back to our families. But all of us wanted to see Thailand. Those of us who had not been there heard all the stories from the old salts about the food, the weather and most important of all, Thai women. Thai women were beautiful, friendly, mysterious and eager to meet American airmen. Six weeks of living in hellhole conditions without the benefit of female companionship was coming to a welcome close. Irv had been talking non-stop for the last two weeks about the charms of the oriental woman. Adding a note of caution, and throwing a bucket of cold water on the whole discussion was our Flight Surgeon, Dr. "Shaky" Akers.

Shaky got his moniker while on a previous rotation to Europe with the squadron. It seems some of the boys got a little frisky one night and pushed over a coke machine. As luck would have it, one of the young Captains was pinned under it. The Captain came out unscathed except for an ugly gash on his forearm. Since it was two o'clock in the morning, with alcohol involved, the guys decided to take him directly to Dr. Akers' room, rather than the base ER. The Doc was unnerved by the whole incident and preceded to stitch up the coke combatant in front of eight witnesses. Maybe it was his rude awakening or just the hooting and loud farting noises from the crowd, but Doc shook as he stitched up the Captain. Hence the name: "Shaky" Akers.

Every time Irv told a story about the magical Thai women he had experienced, Shaky would counter with a gonorrhea-from-hell horror story that was guaranteed to shrink your manhood. These discussions usually occurred while sitting in our Indian O club and consuming large quantities of Indian beer.

Young pilots in those days were decidedly different than today's group. We grew up in the sixties. In the civilian world, it was the era of Woodstock, free love, and smoking dope. As military pilots we had to keep our hair short. None of us would dare to smoke dope. We couldn't afford to lose our wings and get dishonorably discharged. But we loved the music: Jimi Hendrix, Janis Joplin, The Beatles, and The Stones. While we stayed away from the dope, the free love part appealed to some.

For those who attended pilot training on the Mexican border it was the first foray into the international sex scene. Nuevo Laredo was just across the bridge from Laredo, and waiting across that bridge were places like Boys Town (not Father Flanagan's). This Boys Town consisted of several brothels, which contained some very beautiful, reasonable and safe prostitutes. The girls all underwent weekly STD inspections from the Mexican health department. This folded neatly into the philosophy; condoms are for wimps, full speed ahead!

Back in India, when the discussion turned to Thai women and the possibility of picking up some killer STD strain, there was something to think about. Of course, Irv was a bareback guy (no condom). Shaky made a strong case for safety. He even had pictures from medical journals to prove his point. He had my attention.

We flew into U-Tapao, Thailand on a Thursday afternoon and were not scheduled to leave until Sunday morning. The airplanes were in rough shape after six weeks in India. These two days would give the mechanics enough time to prep the planes for the rest of the journey.

The Pattaya Beach area, northwest of the U-Tapao Air Base, was a famous R&R spot for US airmen and that's where we went. The main drag reminded me of a combination of two party places I had been: Bourbon Street in New Orleans and The Strip in Las Vegas. An endless throng of people moving down the street lined on both sides with bars, massage parlors, eateries and brothels. Everything was ablaze with neon lights. Party girls handed out flyers advertising everything from "special" massage to .59-cent beer. Through it all, the faint odor of urine and vomit made this fantasyland all too real.

It seemed like a paradise for the lonely, overworked crewmember. We rolled into Pattiya Beach like Patton's army. It was a true adult's Disneyland but instead of riding Space Mountain we toured Yun's Steam and Cream.

Irv led the charge. To say he went berserk was putting it mildly. His problem was there were too many girls to choose from and most of them were gorgeous, and available. Irv's philosophy was to ask every girl he met to fuck. And I'm not sugarcoating his phrasing. That's what he said: "Hey Honey, wanna fuck?" Of course, using that line on a street full of brothels will get you the right answer every time. Irv would stop at a likely candidate, negotiate a price and get ready to go but then he'd see one across the street who looked better so he'd break from one and sprint to the other. This happened five or six times before he finally committed to one, and off he went. I didn't see him again until the next morning. The rest of us moved from bar to bar trying to maximize our fun before we had to move on.

Waking up the next morning at the BOQ was a truly awful experience. We had spent the night bar hopping and howling at the moon (at least I think that's what I was howling at). We climbed into our beds just before dawn and, mercifully, had no real duties the next day. Somehow we overcame our massive hangovers and started to feel human again by the end of the day. Ah Youth! If I tried something like that today, they'd be hanging a toe tag on me.

Yakota Air Base, Japan, located about 50 kilometers northwest of Tokyo, was the next stop on our journey home. This was an important stop to all of us, especially the young guys. Our older crewmembers had been all over the world and they already had real stereo equipment. We, on the other hand, hadn't been anywhere and had none. This was soon to change.

Japan was the stereo equipment capital of the world and we landed right in the middle of it. The Base Exchange (BX) stocked every major manufacturer's line of stereo equipment and we got a military discount. I was in heaven. I'd been dreaming of getting a real stereo ever since I left college. I dreamed about stereos like Ralphie dreamed of BB guns. Most of my Instructors in pilot training were Southeast Asia vets and came home from their tours with top of the line stereos. So I had a pretty good idea of what I wanted to buy. We certainly hadn't spent any of our paychecks in India so we were ready to buy. I wound up with two sets of speakers (one big, one small); a turntable, a receiver, and a reel-to-reel tape deck, all for $500.

We were able to spend an extra day at Yakota and that was a good thing because we were able to find places to store the stereo equipment along with the cases of wine, guitars, sitars, globe bars, and room screens. The cargo holds of the airplanes now resembled an international furniture bazaar. Since we had three aircraft and six crews, the non-flying crew was stuck in the back with the furniture. The C-130 had webbed seating, which was snapped into position along both sides of the fuselage. The webbed seating was tolerable for a while but soon became uncomfortable. The trick was to claim a nice, flat equipment pallet and layer it with as many blankets as you could find. With all the stuff we were carrying home, space was tight.

Our loadmasters did a great job finding places for all of our treasures. In addition to our personal items, we carried extra tires, engine parts, cases of hydraulic fluid and oil. We carried all the hard to find equipment for a remote operation like Operation Bonny Jack.

When it came time to leave Yakota and make the jump across the Pacific to Elmendorf AFB, Alaska, our airplanes were maxed out. We took as much fuel as we could carry for the long journey across. The flight to Elmendorf was long, boring, and blessedly uneventful. Looking back after 45 years as a pilot, those were my favorite flights, the boring ones.

The best thing about Elmendorf was the bed. We were all so wrung out from the trip; it was heaven just to shower and sleep, and to be back in the USA.

A long flight from Elmendorf to Pope awaited, but at this point we didn't care. We knew we were going home. When we arrived at Pope, the welcome was overwhelming. The whole base turned out. The band played as our aircraft rolled to a stop in front of the bleachers where our families awaited. We had been gone for seven weeks but it had gone by in a flash.

Now we had time to catch up with our families for the next few months. My daughter, Krista, had just celebrated her first birthday in June and the two-month separation brought about some big changes in her appearance. She started walking at 10 months and by the time I returned from India, she was zipping all over the place. With no regrets we said goodbye to Fort Bragg housing. We moved out of Fort Bragg housing and found a nice rental house in Spring Lake, a section of Fayetteville. Everyone was still paranoid about the band of crazed, hippie killers still on the loose waiting to strike at any time. Leaving Fort Bragg was not an option, we had to go.

Chapter 7

Another deployment loomed on the horizon. The C-130 community, like most military units, was gone from home frequently. Our "temporary duties" (TDYs) averaged three per year, with each trip lasting about six to eight weeks. This was hard on family life but we all knew what we were in for when we picked this line of work. We were all willing to do our duty. But that didn't take the sting out of the separations.

The next deployment took the whole squadron to England. Since the end of World War II, the United States has maintained several military bases throughout Europe. Many of these bases housed permanently based Fighter or Reconnaissance units. These units were kept in place to keep our former allies, the communists, from breaching post-war agreements. What the US didn't have permanently in place was airlift capability. All these bases needed resupply and airlift and this was accomplished by regularly rotating the stateside C-130 outfits through Europe. Our turn to go was November of 1971.

There were two rotation bases for the C-130: Mildenhall Air Base in Bury Saint Edmonds, England, and Rhein-Main Air Base in Frankfurt, Germany. The preparation for a rotation starts at least a month prior to departure. For the aircrews all training requirements had to be up to date prior to leaving. Tests had to be taken, check rides flown, passports updated, shot records checked. All legal matters had to be finalized before leaving the US. The families would be on their own for the next two months and they had a network of mutual support to fill the gap during our trip. The maintenance troops had a full schedule of inspections and tests to perform prior to departure also. The more preventative maintenance done now, the more reliably the aircraft would perform overseas. Some of the remote locations we flew into were not places you'd want to experience a breakdown. So the theory was that an ounce of prevention would keep our asses out of trouble later.

We sat through seemingly endless briefings on the European airspace system and its unique rules. Some of the European regulations were similar to the US but there were some important differences and we had to abide by their rules, no excuses accepted. Country borders had to be respected and navigating from one country to another had to be precise.

English is the universal language of aviation, and all controllers, regardless of country, were required to speak in English. That didn't mean we understood them all the time. The controllers would switch back and forth from English to their native tongue depending on which aircraft they were talking to. Flying into Madrid, Spain for example, the controller would speak to us in English and then rapid fire some instructions to an Iberian airliner in Spanish. Sometimes when this happened, pilots would look at each other quizzically and say, "Was that for us?" The theory was, if it was important enough - and it was for us- he would call back.

European countries are very particular about their borders. Transiting their airspace had to be done according to precise navigation and heaven help those who violated them. France, for example, wouldn't let us fly over their airspace most of the time. Looking at a map of Europe, you could see how this could make navigating from say, the UK to Spain, or Denmark to Portugal, difficult. Another major European hot spot was Berlin. Before the Wall fell, navigating in and out of Berlin had to be done along three tight corridors. Straying out of these corridors meant risking a shoot down from a Russian fighter.

We were very much aware of our individual responsibility for following our flight plan and keeping on track. The consequences could be severe. If, for example, our aircraft strayed off course and the controller wrote up a violation, it could have international complications. Countries could ban all military aircraft from their airspace for something we had done. When this type of incident happened, it usually required the head of USAFE (US Air Forces Europe), or even the State Department, to get involved in order to get our clearance reinstated.

Naturally, all this shit ran downhill until it reached the squadron commander who padded this giant, rolling ball and pushed it down the hill on top of the offending crew, squashing them like bugs. The offending crew could face anything from a nuclear ass chewing to being grounded.

The deadline for our departure to Mildenhall was fast approaching. Doreen and Krista were going to spend a month at her Mom's in Philadelphia. Once they were safely in place there, I was ready to go.

Our proposed route was now familiar to me. The first stop was Lajes, Azores. I even knew what kind of wine to buy this time. Prior to leaving Pope, Irv had been briefed on his behavior by the Squadron Commander, Lt Col Shumer. Irv was extremely well behaved for our overnight in Lajes. I personally thought that he was saving all his energy for England. Time would prove me correct.

Mildenhall was a great base. It was small but all the essentials were there. Our home for the next two months was the Bachelor Officer Quarters (BOQ). These rooms were recently refurbished and we each had our own room with a nice bed, small refrigerator, private shower and plenty of storage (just in case we picked up some souvenirs). Right down the street was the Officers Club, our hangout location after every mission. The street in front of our BOQ ran to the front gate, and once through that, England awaited us.

Adjusting to Europe took a bit of time for me. Everything in the US was so large, roomy and pretty new. In England, all was shrunken down. Their houses were tiny, the streets narrow, the cars small and they drove on the wrong side of the road.

Since these C-130 rotations were ongoing, there were a dozen or so cars that were sold by the current squadron to the newcomers. None of these "Rote" cars would be found on the showroom floor. They all ran and were mostly reliable but all had issues.

My buds and I were going for style points so we opted for the big Jaguar. This car looked good but that was all. It had an on-going fuel leak that simply would not stay plugged and the fact that the gas gauge was not reliable meant even a normal journey became exciting. Toss a few beers into the mix, a steering wheel on the right, driving on the left while navigating a roundabout in the rain at night; well, you get the picture. It was an adventure.

And then there was the Lucas electrical system. Anyone who has ever owned an older English car: MG, TR-6, Jaguar, knows what I mean. Lucas, an English company, made the wiring on these cars. Their product was totally unreliable. You'd be riding down a country lane at night and hit a bump and all your lights would go out, both headlights and interior. Hit another bump and the headlights came back on. Another bump and now the interior lights worked. And so it went. Needless to say we all carried flashlights and kept spare ones in the car, along with the spare gas can.

The area around the base was a treasure trove for a history buff like myself. I spent many hours in the town of Ely where there is a magnificent cathedral built by the Benedictine community in 970 A.D. The original founder of Ely cathedral was St. Etheldreda who had quite an unusual marital arrangement. She married at an early age to Tondberht, but she remained a virgin. When her very understanding husband died, she retired to the Isle of Ely, her dowry. In 660, for political reasons, she married Egfrith, the young king of Northumbria who was then only 15 years old. He too, surprisingly agreed that she remain a virgin. Twelve years later, however, Egfrith figured he had waited long enough and demanded his marital rights. The queen refused, so Egfrith offered bribes, to no avail. The queen left him and became a nun. She might have thought about this 15 years earlier and saved this guy a lot of sleepless nights - just sayin'. She founded a monastery in Ely in 673 that became the basis for the Benedictine community.

All the churches in the area, especially Ely Cathedral, had beautiful brass plaques fashioned by medieval craftsmen. We used these plaques to make brass rubbings. One made a rubbing by laying a sheet of paper over the brass and rubbing the paper with various colored crayons. The image produced, if properly done, could be mounted and framed. By the mid 1970s the authorities decided that you could no longer rub the original brasses since careless tourists were wearing them away. Luckily, I got to do a couple of originals before the crackdown.

We flew on a regular basis and none of it was boring for me because it was all new. One trip that appeared regularly on the schedule was called a "Turkey Trot." The US Air Force and Army had several operational bases in Turkey. This changed with the Turkey-Cypriot War in 1974. When this war broke out all but two bases, Incirlik and Izmir, were dramatically reduced. These outlying bases still had a small American presence and regularly needed resupply. A regular Turkey Trot had us hauling a load of engine parts or construction equipment non-stop from Mildenhall to Incirlik Air Base, near Adana, in southern Turkey.

The aircraft would be unloaded and we proceeded to our respective Q's and spent the night. The next two days were spent resupplying some of the smaller, remote stations like Diyarbakir, Mardin, Elazig, and Batman. When I saw that Batman Turkey was one of our destinations I was more than a little curious. Were these Turks really big fans of the American comic book hero or was something else going on here? A little research revealed that Batman was originally a unit of mass in the old Ottoman Empire and that's where the town got its name. But even with this new knowledge, I thought it would be cool to say I lived in Batman, Turkey.

Flying into these places was never a problem as long as the weather was good. When low ceilings or dust storms rolled in, getting on the ground was not a sure thing. While our aircraft had all of the modern instrumentation required to land in the weather, the ground facilities didn't always work like they were supposed to work. Flying into Diyarbakir one dark and stormy night, we set ourselves up for an Instrument Landing

System (ILS) approach. The ILS is a very precise system giving both azimuth and glide slope information bringing you right to the end of the runway. When flown as published, you would break out of the weather, see the runway, and be able to land safely. On one particular night, the weather was not cooperating. Low ceilings, with heavy rain amid thunderstorms covered the entire terminal area. Pilots don't intentionally fly into thunderstorms; we go around them. The C-130 had a decent radar so we had a good picture of the heavy weather. We saw that we would be able to fly an approach to the landing runway and keep clear of the weather. However, we wouldn't see the runway until we got below 400 feet. Most ILS approaches have descent minimums of 200 feet and half-mile visibility. If the ceiling is less than 200 feet or the visibility is less than half a mile, you couldn't legally fly the approach. Your options in such a situation would be to enter a holding pattern somewhere until the weather got better or divert somewhere with better weather. Under the circumstances we had 200 feet to play with.

We set up our approach, tuned and identified the ILS frequency. Each ILS has its own unique frequency and Morse code identifier. We turned the airplane onto final approach and waited for the glideslope to start down. As we started down the glideslope all looked good. We had only come down the glideslope about 300 feet when both needles, azimuth and glideslope, went to full-scale deflection. This dictated we do an immediate go-around, which we did. We then tried to set up for another approach. But now, even the ILS Morse code identifier was not working. The weather was not improving so we had no choice but to head back to Incirlik. We let the air traffic controllers know we had lost the ILS signal and they promised to look into it. The next morning, under sunny skies, we went back to Diyarbakir and made an uneventful landing. We found out from the Operations Officer that a goat had disabled the ILS. Tracing the power lines to the ILS transmitter, they found the main power cable had been chewed through, so much for modern technology.

When we returned to Incirlik that afternoon, we were surprised to learn that we had been kicked out of our BOQs and would have to spend the night at a hotel in the nearby town of Adana. A group of USAFE VIPs was touring the area and had priority for our BOQ rooms. I was not thrilled with this news. Incirlik was not on our list of favorite bases but it was better than Adana. In fact, Adana was what we in the Air Force refer to as a "shithole."

Incirlik was famous for their Turkish crew van drivers. These guys sold pistachio nuts and porn pens. These pens would display several pornographic images as you rotated the barrel, extending or retracting the nib of the pen. These were a must have item for every crewmember and a real conversation starter when we showed them to our friends back in the US. But aside from the pens and the nuts, Incirlik was rough duty.

As bad as Incirlik was, Adana was much worse; at least the hotel we stayed in was. The room keys were giant, dungeon like, with big, carved wooden balls attached to them. I guess they didn't want anyone sneaking off with one in their luggage. It wouldn't fit anyway. At least they put us all on the second floor. Our rooms had small balconies overlooking the street.

My first order of business was a hot shower, so I headed into the bathroom, pulled back the shower curtain, only to discover about four inches of standing green water. After two room changes (the next room had no sheets covering the soiled mattress) I was finally able to clean up and prepare for the evening. We had a delicious meal of roasted goat kabobs. For all I knew I may have eaten the goat that chewed through the ILS cable the night before. We discussed this possibility at dinner but it didn't, in the least, detract from our enjoyment of the meal.

After dinner we left in search of some real Adana nightlife. Turkey is a majority Muslim country but it has a secular government. This meant that alcohol, though strictly controlled, was available. We found a small nightclub not far from the hotel. After several cocktails Herb, Bill and I got up to leave, but Ed Parman insisted on staying. Clint said he would stay with him so we said our goodnights and started back to our rooms.

I was sleeping soundly until I was awakened by loud, angry, Turkish voices coming from the street below the window. I stepped out onto the balcony in the early morning light to find the cause of the commotion and noticed several people pointing up at the second floor. I looked over to see Parman, in his skivvies, peeing off the balcony onto the sidewalk. He had rained on several people on their way to work and they were making their displeasure known. I saw Herb stick his head out of his room and we acknowledged each other with a nod and both raced to Parman's room. We yanked him off the balcony and back to bed. It took some serious sweet-talking to convince the hotel manager not to call the police. We told him that Parman had a medical condition that caused him to sleepwalk. We assured him that Parman would take his medication, thereby allowing the citizens of Adana to proceed to work without getting pissed on.

After four days in Turkey, we were all grateful to be back in Mildenhall. We had a few days off to do some socializing and to catch up on letter writing and laundry. I ran into Irv at the O Club that night and was introduced to his new girlfriend, Angie.

She was a local girl from Thetford, a village not far from the base. She seemed a good match for Irv. She loved to drink and party and, of course, had answered in the affirmative to Irv's standard question to every woman he met: "Hi, do you wanna fuck?" Angie knew Irv was married so she wasn't looking for any long-term commitment, just a good time; and he provided it.

Angie was a beautiful woman and would bring several friends to the Officer's club with her. We called them "The Thetford Girls." The girls had been coming to Mildenhall since long before our arrival. They knew when the C-130 crews were rotating in and made it a point to show up at the club that first week to screen the newcomers for potential boyfriends. Most of these girls weren't as pretty as Angie. Actually, they were all pretty ugly, but available. The kindest phrase one could use when discussing the possibility of having sex with these babes was, "There's not enough beer." They were good sports, however, and could put away their share of the beer.

Chapter 8

One of the most colorful characters in our squadron was Captain Buzz Sawyer. Buzz had been an aircraft commander for three years and had been on several rotations so he was very experienced. He was an Air Force Academy grad affectionately known as a Zoomie. We all admired Buzz but knew that he could be a troublemaker when he overindulged. One night at the O Club, Buzz had knocked back a few too many and was cut off by the bartender. This did not make Buzz happy, and it led to a heated exchange with the bartender. Unable to resolve the issue, the bartender called over the club manager. Buzz would not back down; he wanted a drink and he wanted it now. The club manager escorted him to the door and kicked him out. That worked for about five seconds. Buzz came storming back in and then all hell broke loose.

The club manager and the bartender jumped on his back and Buzz bounced around the room doing his best imitation of a Brahma bull trying to toss off not one, but two riders. Herb and I helped subdue him. We convinced him, for his own wellbeing and for the sake of his Air Force career, that he should go to bed. We escorted him back to his room on the second floor of the BOQ, got his keys away from him, and locked him in his room. Our work having been accomplished, Herb and I returned to the club.

The club manager was so shaken up that he called the SPs (Security Police) and had them stand guard at the main door of the Officer's club just in case Buzz returned. The club manager's hunch was correct.

Buzz did not give up easily. After just a few minutes of lying in bed he decided to head back to the club. Finding his door locked, he figured he'd just go out the window. The drawback to this was that he was on the second floor. Not a problem for Buzz; he was a pilot -- he could fly. He jumped out the window.

Luckily a tree broke his fall. He managed to climb down from the tree. Scratched up but undeterred, he made his way back to the club. He spotted the SPs at the door so he devised an alternate strategy of getting in.

The bar had a large plate-glass window that looked out onto an expansive lawn. Buzz wanted into the bar and the only thing between him and another drink was that window. He jumped through it.

The crash got everyone's attention. From the pile of broken glass and upturned tables and chairs, rose Buzz. Cut and bleeding from a hundred different places, he calmly dusted himself off, walked up to the bar and ordered himself a triple scotch. Buzz spent that night at the base hospital getting stitched up.

That was the last time I saw Buzz until many years later when I was flying for Eastern Airlines. It was the summer of 1986 and I was laying over in Miami. I was relaxing at the hotel bar and looked up to see Buzz sitting across from me. We spent the next couple of hours catching up.

Buzz had left Pope and gone to Vietnam to fly the AC-130 gunship, a truly fearsome flying death machine. The weaponry is mounted to fire from the left side of the airplane. The gunship crew would pick their target and do a standard turn around the target to the left, and it would rain down the lead. It was armed with two 20-millimeter M 61 Vulcan cannons, two Bofors 40-millimeter auto-cannons and one 105-millimeter cannon.

After returning from Vietnam, Buzz left the Air Force and got a job with the CIA. When I met him in Miami he was flying missions for Southern Air Transport, a CIA run air cargo outfit.

About three months after our chance meeting the Sandinistas in Nicaragua shot down a C-123 aircraft flown by Buzz. He was trying to deliver supplies to the Contras. Both pilots and a radio operator were killed in the crash. The only survivor was the loadmaster, Eugene Hasenfus. Hasenfus had disobeyed orders and wore a parachute on the mission. When Sandinista missiles struck the aircraft, Hasenfus jumped out and lived to tell about it.

Things quieted down in Mildenhall after Buzz went on his rampage. During my downtime I kept busy by reading books and articles to pass the time. One book that caught my interest was, "Operation Overflight: A Memoir of the U-2 Incident." Francis Gary Powers wrote it.

The U-2 is a high altitude, single-pilot reconnaissance aircraft that operates above 70,000 feet. It played a vital role in the cold war. Every pilot dreams about flying his or her ultimate aircraft. For me, the U-2 was that aircraft. It was exotic, mysterious, and very difficult to fly. It operated well above the range of both commercial and military aircraft. The U-2 program was extremely difficult to get into, but the rewards of flying this bird made all the work worthwhile. The U-2 pilot performed an important national defense mission and was rewarded with a view of the earth that few people ever had. I admired the mission, the aircraft and people that flew it. Powers' book started me thinking that I could become a U-2 pilot. I didn't have the requirements needed to get into the program but began to plan my future around my holy grail of joining the elite U-2 program.

Our rote car, the leaky Jaguar, always needed some attention. Driving back to the base one night from Surrey, we hit a pothole that disabled the headlights (good old Lucas wiring). We continued down the road waiting for them to come back on but then we hit a large tree branch in the road, which we couldn't see without the lights. The jolt of the impact forced my foot down and through the floorboard. Because we had such nice floor mats, we hadn't noticed that the bottom of the car was rusting away. My right foot was now dangling between the car and the roadway. The driver and the other three passengers thought I had twisted my ankle, not put it through the floor, so on they went. Twisting and turning, I pulled my leg up but it remained jammed in the hole. The interior lighting was also out, so I grabbed my flashlight and lit up the problem. One giant yank and twist and my foot was free, but without my shoe.

Waving my shoeless foot around finally convinced the driver to stop. Everyone piled out, flashlights in hand, scouring the roadway for my shoe. We found it not too far back in the middle of the road. We continued on our way.

The next day we consulted with our maintenance guru, Sgt. McDermott. He was able to scrounge some sheet metal. We cut the pieces to fit over the floorboards and his buddy at the hangar welded them in place. The Jag would live on. We had to keep the car in running condition so we could pass it on to the next rotation group. If we didn't, we would lose our investment.

Chapter 9

As we geared up for our next trip, our Aircraft Commander, Herb, had to return to Pope to be with his wife after she underwent an emergency appendectomy. His replacement was Mike Langley. Mike was a sharp pilot and an easygoing guy. We got along well.

The next mission was to the island of Crete in the Mediterranean. The US Navy has a base on the island at Souda Bay, on the north side. The plan was to fly down there non-stop, deliver our cargo, and spend the night. Just as we began our descent, the number four-engine oil pressure started dropping out of the safe range. We throttled back on Number 4 but kept it running. The landing was uneventful.

Maintenance determined that one of the oil pressure transmitters had gone bad. They needed a day to have it repaired. It meant we got to spend an extra night on the island. It was a great place to be stuck.

There were several excellent restaurants within a short drive from the base. The restaurants specialized in fresh lamb dishes and what is now known as the "Mediterranean Diet." Both nights we feasted on the wonderful food and the delicious Greek wine.

Crete was the best place to buy a genuine Flokati rug. This is a handmade rug made from shag wool. The rug's backing is also wool and the shag emerging from the backing can be up to six inches long. After the rug is woven, it's placed in a cold river to fluff the shag. I bought one and still have it today.

With our airplane fixed and shopping complete, it was time to head back to Mildenhall. Just before departure, we received a message asking us to stop in Athens to pick up an Army General and his aide. We made the quick stop in Athens, boarded our passengers, and were off to England.

Before our arrival, the weather had deteriorated at Mildenhall. The English weather is challenging; especially when the fog rolls in. This fog bank covered the entire southern half of the country. This happened to be where all of the bases were. We checked the Mildenhall weather just prior to leaving Athens and even though there were low ceilings and visibility, it was good enough to try an approach and landing there. The problem was that it was trending worse and it was widespread. We loaded as much fuel as possible and listed our alternate airport as Ramstein Air Base, Germany. When the weather drops below certain ceiling and visibility minimums an alternate airport must be listed in the flight plan. This was the closest base with decent weather so we would head there if we couldn't land at our destination.

When we arrived at Mildenhall the weather was just at minimums: 200' ceiling and a half mile visibility. Most of today's airliners are computer controlled and flown mostly on autopilot. The normal takeoff and landing are done manually but when the weather is bad, the autopilot can take the aircraft right down to touchdown. After touchdown and rollout, the pilot disconnects the autopilot and taxis clear of the runway. Using the autopilot enables today's crews to land in much worse weather than the C-130 in 1972 ever could.

The C-130 instrument approaches and landings were hand-flown by either the Aircraft Commander or the co-pilot. Both were fully qualified to take the aircraft down to minimums.

Floating through this solid weather at night was an eerie sensation. Managing the exterior lighting was critical in accomplishing a successful bad weather approach and landing. Turning the lights on prior to that was blinding in the dense fog. We decided to keep the landing lights off until the runway came into view. There are also rotating beacons that increase the visibility of the plane in flight and warn ground personnel when engines are operating. Sometimes the red beacon lights bounce off the clouds and can cause vertigo. We hadn't felt any effects from the rotating beacon yet so we left it on.

Mike began the first approach. We stayed on course and glide path. We were in the weather at 1000 feet, at 500 feet and finally at 200 feet, still in the weather, no runway in view. We executed a missed approach.

Mike set up for the next approach and it was now my turn to fly. While turning for the next approach, Mike started complaining of vertigo. I continued to fly as he sat back and closed his eyes. I started feeling a bit wobbly myself so I opted to turn off the beacon. My approach looked like an instant replay of his. It was on course and glide path all the way down but the weather never broke. We did another missed approach.

There was enough fuel to do three or four approaches and still make it to Ramstein. As we climbed out and set up for the next one my vertigo increased. Mike now felt better and I transferred control back to him.

Mike started in on the approach. The air traffic controller reported the visibility had increased slightly so our hopes were high for this one. All remained the same right down to minimums but just as we started going around again, a portion of the runway became visible. We were in no position to land so we continued with the missed approach.

Vertigo is insidious and after flying approaches in the weather it can come on quickly. The climbs, descents, turns, accelerations and decelerations, can significantly affect the inner ear. Mike's vertigo came back quickly. Vertigo affects the inner ear, which affects balance. Mike had the false sensation that the aircraft was turning left but we were actually flying straight and level. Many inexperienced pilots try to correct the false sensation of turning by rolling in the opposite direction. The pilot has to disregard his perception and believe the instruments. Many a pilot has spiraled himself into a smoking hole following this false perception and not following his instruments.

Since my vertigo had stopped Mike turned the controls back to me. We decided to try one more approach before diverting to Ramstein. Just as we reached minimums, the lead-in lights and the first few runway lights came into view. I followed the glideslope down and landed about 1500 feet down the runway.

The fog at the end of the runway was much worse than at the approach end. When we cleared the runway, the tower called and asked our position. We gave him the taxiway identifier and requested a follow-me truck to lead us to our ramp. The soup was so thick we couldn't see the edges of the taxiway, which was 150 feet wide. The follow-me truck found us in the fog and led us back to our ramp. The General was very glad to be back on the ground. He thanked us profusely for delivering him safely, walked off the airplane to his waiting staff car, and we never saw him again.

We met up at the O club later that night and discussed the flight over a few cold ones. We learned that our airplane was the only one to make it into Mildenhall that night. With the way the fog was moving, if we had arrived just five minutes later we wouldn't have seen anything on that fourth approach.

We had the next few days off and Mike and I decided to take the train to London for some sightseeing. Mike had been there several times but this visit would be my first. We managed to see most of the popular sights including St. Paul's Cathedral, the Tower of London, the crown jewels, Big Ben and Parliament. My personal favorite was

221B Baker Street, the residence of Sherlock Holmes. As a boy I had read everything by Holmes' creator, Sir Arthur Conan Doyle. There is no real 221B Baker Street but it's marked nonetheless, as Sherlock Holmes address. Just standing in front his fictional address was thrilling to me and I could imagine his adventures. It made the whole trip worthwhile.

We wanted to wrap up our day by visiting a traditional English pub. Ye Olde Cheshire Cheese on Fleet Street looked perfect. It enticed us by its claim to be the oldest pub in London. The pub may have been old but the beer was certainly fresh and it was a pleasant way to finish off a day of strenuous sightseeing.

There were too many things we hadn't done in London but our flight schedule demanded our return to base. London wasn't going anywhere, but we were. We put more sightseeing there on our "to do" list.

Chapter 10

Next up for us was a joint training exercise at the naval air station in Naples, Italy. These joint training exercises are regularly scheduled events. They focus on integrating the actions of different branches of the military. US Air Force units, for example, work well together but coordination with the Navy or the Army was required because each service had its own particular way of doing things. The joint exercises stressed communication and cooperation.

Two aircraft and crews would participate in a two-day exercise. We would be carrying a load of simulated aircraft missiles to be used by Navy fighter jets. These were reusable, dummy missiles that would be loaded on the participating fighters. When the exercise was over, they would be loaded back on the C-130s for the return to Mildenhall. Our job was simply to deliver the missiles, head for the layover, and return to the UK when the exercise finished.

This sounds fairly simple until you add in "The terror cab ride from hell."

Naples is known as the city of crazy drivers, trash, and Camorra (the local Mafia). The city has beautiful views of Mount Vesuvius and a gorgeous bay but it also has an ongoing trash problem, which is linked to the Mafia. Waste companies are Mafia owned. They use trash collection to extort money from the government.

The regions' dumps fill to capacity and with nowhere to put it, the trash piles up and a state of emergency is declared. City government officials use the state of emergency to quickly award contracts that otherwise would have to be checked by anti-racketeering legislation.

The Mafia-owned waste management companies dispose of the trash anywhere they can - out in the open air or at already full dumps. There were attempts to build new incinerators and open new landfills but companies building them either couldn't finish the job or magistrates stopped the work pending ongoing criminal investigations.

Back to the crazy drivers. No one knows how their reputations got started but it is a well-deserved one. Maybe it's because they had to bob and weave around all the garbage piles.

After we unloaded our aircraft, the transit coordinator for our exercise called for taxis for the two crews, 10 people in total. He told us the ride to the hotel would take around 20 minutes in normal traffic. If Naples traffic is anything, it's not normal.

Three taxis arrived around 15 minutes later. All were small Fiats. We put four of the smallest guys in one cab. The luggage wouldn't fit in the trunk so it was lashed to the rack on the back. The other two taxis held three each with a similar arrangement of the luggage. Our driver spoke not a word of English and the only Italian we knew was ciao, bella, and arrivaderci.

The drivers all looked the same – short and hairy with cigarette packs rolled up in their sleeves. They looked vaguely like Mussolini. They may have been related but we didn't pursue the point; we only wanted to get to the hotel. We showed them the hotel name and address and they nodded eagerly, indicating they knew where it was.

Once the drivers knew the destination and everything was loaded in the cabs, all hell broke loose. Each driver raced to his cab shouting and gesturing to each other in what sounded like insulting terms. Apparently, these pint-sized Mario Andrettis had wagered on who could reach the hotel first. The race was on and the passengers were merely along for the ride. We flew down the street, tires screeching. Traffic signals and stop signs were meaningless. They didn't even bother to stay on the street. When they came to a blocked intersection, they hopped up on the sidewalk, scattering pedestrians in all directions. We were all too terrified to speak, or move. Without seat belts our only hope was that our tight fit would keep us from flying out of the cab in an accident. When one of us finally spoke up, the driver pointed to the other cabs and mumbled something in Italian. If I were to guess, he was saying: "Hey, leave me alone, I have to keep up with these two."

As we slid to a stop in front of the hotel, we were all wild-eyed and shaken. Our cab came in second so our driver jumped out and yelled at the winner; all the while counting out the money he lost on the bet. The scene was repeated for the third cab. After unloading our luggage and getting paid, the three pocket rockets hopped back in their Fiats and roared off into the night.

The rest of our time in Naples wasn't nearly as exciting as the cab ride but we still enjoyed ourselves. I was able to fit in a trip to the Naples National Archaeological Museum. The museum was full of sculptures and artifacts collected from Pompeii and Herculaneum. And no trip to Naples would be complete without a real Napoli pizza.

The time to return to Pope was rapidly approaching. There was only one more mission to fly before heading home. It was a fairly routine trip but to an interesting destination. Our job was to move an Army colonel, his wife, and their furniture from Rhein-Main, Germany to Bizerte Sidi Ahmed, Tunisia. The colonel was assigned to the US Embassy in Tunisia and we were his United Van Lines. The whole crew looked forward to this one because none of us had ever been to Africa.

The weather that day was perfect: no clouds, no wind, and great visibility. Upon landing in Tunisia we were greeted by a representative of the US Embassy. He had arranged an elaborate open-air luncheon for us. The luncheon was set on a hill overlooking the city. A large native-crafted canopy shaded us. The meal consisted of native Tunisian dishes including spicy mutton, lablabi, (a thick soup made from chickpeas and garlic), fresh fish, vegetables, fruits, nuts and couscous, the national dish of Tunisia. The food was delicious and spicy. The Tunisians use a spice mix in their cooking called "Tabil" (pronounced "table"). Tabil is made from a mixture of garlic, cayenne pepper, caraway seeds and coriander. Once mixed together, the tabil is then dried in the sun. We were all surprised by how hot the food was. We had to blunt the fiery spices with traditional Tunisian oven-baked bread and lots of water. With nothing pressing scheduled for us after our furniture run, we savored this exotic meal and then headed back to the UK.

As fate would have it, the entire squadron was in base at Mildenhall on New Year's Eve in 1971. We were set to leave in four days so it was a perfect opportunity for a party. The event could have been compared to "Animal House." It was just as raucous but without the togas. The music was loud, the liquor flowed freely and we welcomed in the New Year in fine style.

The next morning, the base held its annual New Year's Day Parade with the Mildenhall Base Band and Color Guard leading the way. Every permanent organization on base was represented in the parade. Since we were there on temporary duty, we wouldn't be marching, only watching.

Irv and Angie had been up all night in heavy party mode. The parade route ran right under our windows in the BOQ. Irv had bought one of those giant alpine horns, the kind in the commercial for "Ricolla" cough drops. The Base Commander and his wife were in a convertible following the band and color guard. Irv and Angie wanted to participate in the festivities so they hung out of the windows with Irv blowing the horn and Angie holding the other end. Just blowing this gigantic horn was bad enough, but to put icing on this parade cake, both of them were stark naked.

The parade was rolling along smoothly until Irv started in with his horn. Everything came to a halt as all eyes focused on the bizarre pair of nudists hanging out of the second floor windows. The Base Commander's wife nearly fainted. The Base Commander himself was red-faced. He was pointing up at Irv and yelling instructions. He was extremely pissed. Several members of the squadron rushed into Irv's room and yanked both of them from the windows. Once they disappeared from view, the parade rolled on.

The next morning, Irv found himself on the carpet of the Squadron Commander enduring a royal ass chewing. He was put on the equivalent of double secret probation and told to behave himself, or else.

We tied up our loose ends at Mildenhall. This included selling our leaky Jag to the incoming group. The Jag was actually in better shape than when we bought it. We at least made our money back. Everything was loaded onto the airplanes and we headed back across the Atlantic to Pope.

Chapter 11

As much as we loved Mildenhall, it was great to be back home. The next six months were spent catching up with our families. It was a beautiful time to be in North Carolina. The springtime weather is unbeatable and it's a great place to be if you liked outdoor activities. Seven of us squadron co-pilots bought motorcycles, actually high horsepower dirt bikes. These 250cc tree climbers were tough, powerful bikes for use off-road. Fort Bragg is one of the largest military installations in the country with thousands of acres of forestland. Woven through these forests are miles of trails used by the Army to train their tank crews. The tank trails made perfect off-road opportunities for us. We would meet once a week to ride the powerful dirt bikes. Up, down, around and around we went for hours in the North Carolina woods. Every boy's dream fully realized, racing around a pristine wilderness with your buddies trying not to break your neck.

A week before our next rotation, I walked out of my house for one last ride before we left for Europe. I never got to make that ride. Some bastard had stolen my bike and I was grounded.

Before we left for Europe, all squadron members were called to a mandatory meeting. As is normal in the military, several rumors were in the air about the purpose of the meeting. Some thought it meant the cancellation of our rotation. Others said it meant a massive cutback or transfer of aircraft to other units. None of this proved true. The meeting was called to introduce the new squadron commander, Lt. Col. Benny Fioritto. Col. Benny, as we knew him, was a legend in the C-130.

Benny had pioneered several operational innovations in the C-130 including LAPES drops and several short-field landing techniques. Benny was a pilot's pilot. He rose up through the ranks due to his hard work and innovative thinking. If it ever had been done in a C-130, Benny had done it. He also looked out for his guys. He stood up for, and protected, his pilots. Young pilots on overseas rotations can get "frisky" and wind up in trouble with local authorities. He knew what training and dedication it took to accomplish a mission and he went to bat for us. That didn't mean we had carte blanche. We were expected to fly by the book and God help us if we crossed the line. None of us wanted to either disappoint him or face his wrath, so we played by the rules. But we also played. We were expected to blow off steam, within reason.

Irv was so excited about our new commander that he set about creating a calling card for squadron pilots. He thought it would be a real icebreaker with the ladies. He insisted on designing and financing the cards himself. He promised to have them ready soon. He didn't have enough time to finish them before we left for Germany so he arranged for his wife to ship them to us.

The pre-departure routine remained the same as last time with the only major difference being our destination. Now we were bound for

Rhein-Main Air Base in Frankfurt Germany. Rhein-Main was a dual use facility. Civilian aviation was on one side of the field, the military on the other.

Our BOQ set up in Rhein-Main was unique. It was a round building, two stories high with rooms around the perimeter and a large open rotunda in the center. Every rotation had its "must have" item for the pilots. These trends started when one or two crews went out on a trip and brought back something unique. It then became the rage. On our last rotation, it was porn pens from Turkey and rugs from Crete. This time it was the Italian cap pistol.

Shortly after arriving in Rhein-Main, one of our crews went down to Aviano, Italy (the home of the Globe Bar) for an overnight. One of the pilots saw cap pistols for sale in Pisa and brought a half dozen back. They were incredibly realistic looking. The pistol was a replica of a snub-nosed .38 caliber revolver. You could break it open just like the real gun but instead of inserting bullets, you'd insert a plastic, six-shot cap ring. These caps were loud and they rarely misfired.

Everyone wanted one; they would be perfect for an after-hours gunfight at the Officer's Club. Soon, we were all armed, but not so dangerous.

One afternoon, Benny called a pilot's meeting to be held in our Q rotunda. Benny and the Ops Officer, Sweats Tollefson, set up in the middle with all the pilots in a circle around them on the second floor balcony. The word had been passed; we were going to ambush the Boss. The meeting began quietly enough with Benny and Sweats reviewing some operational notes about European flying. Other boring, miscellaneous crap was covered until; finally, the meeting was about to end. Someone shouted, "NOW," and we all drew our pistols and started firing down on Benny and Sweats. The noise in that enclosed rotunda was deafening. Sweats hit the deck unsure of what the hell was going on. Benny just stood there smiling throughout the fusillade. When all of our caps were spent, Benny calmly reached inside his flight suit, pulled out his cap gun and fired back at us. We all laughed hysterically as we stood there in the gun smoke-filled rotunda. Our ears rang from the hundreds of rounds fired. Benny went right along with the joke. A lesser man would have court-marshaled all of us.

Colonel Benny Fioritto was Italian. His parents had emigrated to the U.S. from Sicily when Benny was a baby. I found all this out when a mission to Sicily came open for us. One airplane and crew were to fly to Sigonella Air Base in Sicily, drop off some parts for the Navy, and return the next day. Our crew was selected but there was a caveat; Benny wanted to come with us. His family had come from the town of Catania. Since this town was near the base, Benny would have an opportunity to see his birthplace and visit with some relatives who stayed behind. Benny was a hands-on Commander. He sat in the back for most of the flight down there but he wanted the landing at Sigonella. He and Mike switched seats and Benny and I brought her into Sigonella. His Aunt and Uncle met Benny and took him into town. He returned several hours later and took us all into town for drinks and dinner. The tavern he chose was ordinary looking, but the people inside were anything but ordinary. They all had known Benny's family. They were very proud that one of their own had gone to the U.S., been very successful, and now was back among them. We couldn't buy a drink all night.

Chapter 12

Things were quiet back at Rhein-Main. Our crew took extended trips to Greece, Turkey, Spain and Portugal. Late one evening, Irv came into my room highly excited. He had received our squadron business cards. The front of the card had a drawing of a cartoon C-130 with a giant handlebar mustache on its nose. Wrapped around the fuselage of this cartoon 130 were crisscrossed ammunition belts. The airplane was wearing a Mexican sombrero. Underneath the squadron designation was the phrase "Fioritto's Banditos."

I was very impressed with the card and told Irv that I liked it. Irv said: "If you think that's good, turn it over." On the flipside were the letters LAGNAF. No explanation, just letters. I looked at Irv for an explanation.

"That's our squadron theme, it's like Semper Fi or Veritas." he said.

"I don't ever recall seeing LAGNAF in any Latin I've ever read."

"Oh that's not Latin. It means Let's All Get Naked And Fuck," he said.

I was speechless. He was handing out these cards to everybody he met, including the Base Commander and the Chaplin. He was also handing them out off base to German civilians. This had all the makings of an international incident. Irv didn't care, anything to pick up chicks. My only hope was that he wasn't volunteering to de-cypher the cryptic letters on the back.

We managed to finish our rotation without any major crises. Irv did get into a minor scuffle at the O Club one night. The Base Supply Officer and his wife were having a drink at the bar when Irv passed them one of his cards. The wife just happened to flip the card over and wanted to know what the letters on the back of the card stood for. So Irv told her. Her husband leapt up and snatched the cards out of Irv's hand. Irv grabbed them back and both of them wound up rolling on the floor, fighting for possession. The other patrons intervened and a major fistfight was avoided.

Chapter 13

After our return to Pope, I prepared myself for my next career move, to the left seat, as Aircraft Commander. Technically, flying the C-130 is about the same whether you're in the left or right seat. The only difference is which hand flies and which one operates the throttles. It does take time to transition but after doing it for a few hours the new seat feels natural. The big job difference was the responsibility. The Aircraft Commander is ultimately responsible for the airplane, crew, passengers, and cargo. He needs input from his crew but he alone must answer for all. Several weeks of ground school were also required. As 1973 rolled in I had my hands full with training school. I was lucky with scheduling and the weather and was able to finish up by the end of February. I liked this feeling. As Mel Brooks said: "It's good to be the King."

My first mission as a brand new Aircraft Commander was a sweet one. The U.S. Navy was conducting torpedo tests in the Bahamas, near Andros Island. They would launch the torpedoes, without explosives, at dummy targets. They would retrieve the spent torpedoes and ship them to a testing facility in Florida, near Patrick AFB. Our job was to fly to Andros Island, load up the torpedoes, and fly them over to Patrick AFB, near Cape Kennedy. It was a short, 45-minute flight each way and we did this once a day, for a week. Most of the day we were free to roam around in the beautiful sunshine. We spent many hours touring Cape Kennedy, eating seafood, drinking beer, and laying in the sun. All in all, not bad duty.

Chapter 14

Back at Pope, there were rumors of an exotic TDY coming to our squadron. In short order these rumors became facts. Sub Saharan Africa was in crisis. A severe drought was rapidly expanding the desert and driving the nomadic people, the Tuaregs, south. The Tuaregs were sheep and goat herders and their normal water supplies were disappearing fast. The herds were dying and the Tuaregs would soon follow. The squadron asked for volunteers and I jumped at the opportunity. Three airplanes would go, two to Mali and one to Chad. Two crews were assigned to each aircraft for a total of six.

My aircraft would be going to Bamako, Mali, located in northwestern Africa. On my crew were: Co pilot Jack Taylor, Navigator Ed (Headwind) Hill, Flight Engineer Albert Moses, and Loadmaster Billy Tate. Jack was a very experienced co pilot who had already been on two rotations and he played a mean guitar. Major Hill earned his nickname while at Pope. He was flying a large triangular flight pattern one day and the crew noticed that every leg had a headwind. They jokingly blamed this on Major Hill and the nickname stuck. SSgt Moses was one of the sharpest engineers in the squadron. He arrived at Pope in January 1973 right out of training school. Sgt. Billy Tate had been on the Rhine-Main rotation the previous year.

We left Pope and the first stop was our old standby, Lajes, Azores. We spent the night there, refueled, and left Lajes the next morning for Africa. The weather was beautiful and clear all the way. Our route took us directly to the west coast of Africa near Dakar, Senegal. From there we turned directly for Mali.

Bamako is located in the southwestern part of Mali. What struck me most about seeing this part of Africa for the first time was the brown flatness of everything. You could see an occasional village with conical grass huts scattered about but not much of anything else. Bamako itself stood in stark contrast to the surrounding countryside. We could see its buildings from miles out. The city straddled both sides of the Niger River. Just south of the city was the airport. Navigation aids and air traffic control facilities were primitive in sub-Saharan Africa in 1973. All this flying would be visual flight rules (VFR). This meant that if you could see it, you could go. These flying rules were the same ones we used in Gauhati, so we were experienced in this type of flying.

As we made our approach to the Bamako airport we could see that the city consisted of mostly flat-roofed single story structures with one big exception. There was one high-rise building, the Hotel De L'Amitier. This would be our home for the next six weeks.

After landing we taxied to our parking ramp and were met by a delegation from the Malian government. They gave us a warm welcome and repeatedly thanked us for coming to their aid in this time of crisis. We climbed on a large, ancient bus that pulled up to the aircraft and we were off to the Hotel De L'Amitier.

The view from the ground confirmed what we had seen from the air: flat, brown and dusty. The hotel was the exception. It was 15 stories high and so new that it wasn't completely finished yet. We maneuvered our equipment and luggage around sawhorses and sand piles and finally checked into our rooms. I was pleasantly surprised by the opulence of my room. It had air conditioning, a bath with a tub-shower combination, a toilet that actually worked, a beautiful double bed, and the most unusual chair coverings I'd ever seen. The chair and small sofa were covered with real animal skins. The chair was done in zebra; the sofa in leopard skin. This was definitely not the PETA suite. I had a great view of the entire city from the 12th floor.

We cleaned up and I met Jack and Ed for drinks. We noted that there were a lot of candles around the hotel. After the sun went down we found out why. Electricity was an iffy proposition in Mali. Sometimes it worked, most of the time it didn't. After a nice candle-lit dinner in the hotel restaurant, we adjourned to our rooms. Just prior to leaving the restaurant the electricity came back on so we were able to use the elevators. I opted for the stairs, just in case.

After getting back to my room I started reading a book that Jack had shared with me. I had to read by candlelight since the power went out... again. The book was, "The Exorcist." Now I'm not easily rattled by spooky stories, but there was something about sitting in a room alone, in the middle of Africa, reading this ghastly story by candlelight. I was on edge all night and didn't sleep at all.

One piece of good news was that the hotel had priority on the electric grid. It was the last to lose it and the first to get it back. But when the power went out, the blackness was total. Looking out my window I saw a vast sea of nothingness with only an occasional twinkle from the scattered peasant huts below my window.

Chapter 15

The borders of present day Mali were drawn in 1890 when the country was known as French Sudan. Mali remained a French colony until it achieved independence in 1960.

Our mission was to deliver grain to small outposts on the edge of the Sahara. Distribution points for the grain were set up around five destination airstrips. We were part of a massive international relief effort. Successive dry years killed both crops and livestock. The Sahara crept southward and thousands of people faced starvation. Existing means of transportation couldn't move the grain inland quickly enough. Most waterways were unsuitable for barges to reach the northern areas. The only workable solution was to airlift the grain in to where it was needed.

Those hardest hit by this drought were the Tuaregs. They lead a nomadic, pastoral life in the Sahara desert. In 1973, the severe drought conditions drove the Tuaregs out of their traditional grazing lands and pushed them south where they sought food and water.

My lasting impression of the operation was the unremitting heat and sand. During the day, the temperature rose into the triple digits. The highest I witnessed was 116 degrees. It would cool off somewhat from evening through early morning however, and this had a direct effect on how much we could carry. There were two launches per day.

The 6:00 A.M. flight carried 13 ½ metric tons of grain and the afternoon sortie carried 11 ½ metric tons. The load difference was due to the outside air temperature. The cooler temperatures allowed us to carry a greater load. Cooler air was denser, which meant more lift.

We were based in Bamako, and all of our destinations were in the north: Timbuktu, Goundam, Gao, Nioro, and Nara. All these destinations had runways consisting of dirt and a red, residual product of rock decay called laterite.

All the airports had control towers. This was good -- except for the language barrier and faulty equipment. The tower operators were supposed to communicate with us in English, the international language of aviation. But French was the official language of Mali and its natives rarely got to use English until we arrived. As time went on their English got better and so did our French.

The control towers used old radios that had high failure rates. Many times the radio operator's transmission would just stop in mid-sentence. Sometimes they fixed the problem and came back on the air, sometimes not.

Though there were radio operators in the towers there were no air traffic controllers. In the U.S. and in Europe, air traffic controllers had all the planes on radar screens and guided the traffic to avoid conflicts with other planes. When we were flying in Mali in the 70's there was no radar. Once cleared for takeoff by the tower, we were on our own; not only to navigate to our destination, but also to avoid other airplanes. We never had any near misses, or near hits, as George Carlin called them. We used the "see and avoid" principle of flight and self sequenced for every approach and landing.

Sand was a constant problem. Sometimes it reduced visibility down to zero. With the drought conditions and the Sahara being so close, the sand went from ground level to 20,000 feet. The sand also affected our airplanes. It peeled most of the paint off the propellers and the leading edges of the wings. The sand would even work its way into our aircraft air-conditioning packs. Halfway through our six week stay, the air-conditioning and pressurization systems were shot. The conditions were so oppressive we stopped wearing flight suits. "T" shirts and shorts became the uniform of the day.

Our longest flight was to Gao, about 2 ½ hours. The shortest was Nara, about 30 minutes. The weather reports were unreliable. Even our Air Force meteorologists couldn't predict what the sand would do. We would load up, take off, and head to our destination. If we could see enough to land, we did. If not, we'd turn around and go back to base.

Most of the northern runways were short. This required us to perform a specific type of approach and landing known as a short field landing. The glide slope was very steep. The aircraft was configured with full flaps and minimum speed. The aiming point for touchdown was between 500' and 1000' down the runway. Once on the ground, we applied maximum breaking and pulled the props into reverse. When the sand kicked up from our reversing props and enveloped the aircraft, we'd bring the props out of reverse and the aircraft emerged from the sand cloud, at taxi speed.

Once on the ground, we were met by a group of laborers, typically around 50 men, with trucks standing by to transport the grain. Without heavy equipment the sacks of grain had to be offloaded by manual labor. The workers would enter the aircraft through the aft ramp and a truck would park right up against the back of the airplane. The workers were not big men. They were all very thin but very strong. Each bag of grain weighed from 80 to 100 pounds. Two workers would grab the ends of the sack and lift it on to the back of a "runner." These "runners" would carry the sacks to the truck where two men would relieve them of the grain and stack it in the truck. The workers were fast, off loading the plane in less than 30 minutes.

Chapter 16

Timbuktu was one of the locations where we delivered grain. Prior to going to Mali, I thought Timbuktu was a fictional remote city like Shangri-La. But the city was real. The Tuaregs founded it in the 11th century.

Timbuktu attracted both scholars and merchants. It became a scholarly center and important trade port where goods from west and north Africa were exchanged. Salt from mines in the north was traded for gold mined in the south. Black and Arab scholars flocked to this thriving hub and established several important libraries there.

When our sister ship got stuck in Timbuktu, our crew headed up there with a load of grain, maintenance technicians, and spare parts to fix the other aircraft. One of the stuck plane's engines wouldn't start. We hoped the two techs plus our two flight engineers could come up with a solution. The problem with the engine couldn't get solved by the afternoon so we had to spend the night and give it another go in the morning.

The local government assigned a guide to arrange transportation, hotel rooms, and even dinner reservations. His name was Mustafa and he spoke broken, but understandable English. Our rooms in Timbuktu were not as nice as our rooms in Bamako, but they were clean. Some of us even had hot water.

We gathered in the small lobby of the hotel. Mustafa did a head count and led us down the street to the restaurant he had chosen. I don't recall the name of the restaurant but I'll never forget the food. The first course was some kind of bird egg cooked in what looked like clippings from my lawn mower. Then came sorghum and small, rock-like potatoes (best guess). The main course was a meat dish. The texture of the meat was unfamiliar to me and was heavily spiced. I asked our guide what it was. Mustafa simply said, "It is small beast." I left it at that.

The next morning it was back to the airport to try to solve the mystery of the non-starting Number 3 engine. Getting that airplane back in the air was critical. The more grain we could deliver, the more lives we could save.

The Flight Engineer from the crew of the stuck plane was SMSgt Ed Hinesmann. He was the most experienced and trusted engineer, not only in our squadron but also in the entire wing at Pope, which consisted of three squadrons. Our Flight Engineer, Albert Moses, and Hinesmann went to work on the problem. They had run through every start problem scenario without success. Then in a stroke of luck Moses discovered the problem.

The C-130, like most airliners and turboprops, has "T" handles for use in shutting down the engine in emergencies, like engine fires. Pulling the T-handle would cut off fuel, oil and hydraulic pressure to the engine. During an engine fire, this T-handle would flash red and a loud warning bell would sound. What Moses discovered was Number 3 T-handle had been pulled out. The difference between full out position and full in was only a half-inch. No one knew how the handle had been pulled out. But when they pushed it in, the engine started up immediately. Hinesmann was humbled and mortified that he missed such a simple solution.

Malians had many ailments; among which were malaria, dysentery, lack of clean water, and easy access to good medical care. In 1973, Mali had the shortest life span of any country on earth, 34.4 years. A large segment of the population was affected by onchocerciasis, otherwise known as river blindness. It's a parasitic disease caused by a roundworm infection that is transmitted through the bite of a black fly. The roundworm larva are introduced through the bite and spread throughout the body. This causes severe itching and can destroy optical tissue.

In spite of this and other daily difficulties of life in a dirt-poor country, the Malians were a joyful people. All the ones that I met were friendly, outgoing and appreciative of our efforts in their behalf. Every time I flew, regardless of destination, I would receive an invitation to someone's home. Due to our schedule, I was only able to accept two of these invitations during our six-week stay. On both occasions I was impressed with their joy for living and their warmth.

On those rare days off we loved to explore the streets of Bamako. One day as we walked along a few blocks from our hotel we noticed a tall tree with hundreds of long black pods, about a foot long, hanging from the branches. A crowd of small children had gathered at the base of the tree. They had several rudimentary slingshots and were attempting to knock the pods from the tree. We watched as an eight or nine-year-old boy aimed his slingshot and hit his target, knocking the pod to the ground. He was very proud of his accomplishment and brought the pod over to show us. These pods turned out to be sleeping, foot-long bats. The little guy laid the bat at our feet and proceeded to slit its throat with a piece of a broken coke bottle. I knew food was scarce in Mali and now I knew just how scarce. These little guys weren't shooting for sport; they were shooting for food. As I looked down on the ground at this giant, bleeding bat, I thought about my meat dish in Timbuktu. Small beast, indeed.

The unremitting heat and the daily grind were having an effect on us. Trying to keep the airplanes flying while maintenance issues plagued us caused a lot of stress. We were committed to doing the best we could but, above all else, it had to be safe. If we were able to press on safely in spite of a maintenance problem we would. A good example of this was when our plane had an inoperative air conditioning system. There was a part coming in from Pope but it would take two weeks to arrive. We operated without it until the part arrived. It was uncomfortable but safe.

The six-week stay in Africa was coming to an end and we all yearned to see the states again.

In spite of the hardships, I treasured my time in Mali. We made a real difference in the lives of thousands of people. They needed our help and we came through for them. We learned a few valuable lessons while there. We learned that life is precious, embrace it; every human being has value no matter what his background or what's in his pocket; when the job is important enough, find a way to get it done, despite hardships. These lessons stayed with me throughout my professional and personal life.

The situation in Mali today is still unsettled. Since January of 2012, the country has been fighting a war with separatist forces consisting of Tuareg rebels and radical Islamists. These rebel forces are concentrated in the northern part of the country. The northern area contains the regions of Timbuktu, Kidal and Gao, which are the least populated and most arid regions of the country.

The rebels declared the secession of a new state, Azawad. In 2012, in response to the increasing Islamist threat to the country, French paratroopers, together with Malian forces, recaptured most of the north. The fighting continues today with no resolution in sight.

PART II

Chapter 1

I hadn't been back at Pope very long when an interesting career opportunity came up. As much as I enjoyed flying the C-130, I always had my antennae up for other flying jobs. I didn't want a specific airplane. I was looking for an exciting airplane attached to a rewarding job. In the Air Force, such jobs were uncommon.

Tactical Air Command (TAC) had received a request from Air Training Command (ATC) for experienced C-130 pilots to become Instructor Pilots. Up until then, most Instructor Pilots had come from the ranks of new pilot graduates. Headquarters at ATC thought that it would be a good idea to mix in experienced pilots with the current crop of Instructors. The instructor job sounded interesting but I needed the right airplane to make it a go for me.

I wanted into the program only if I could fly the T-38. The T-38 is a pilot's dream. It's a two-engine jet, white, supersonic, sleek, front and back seating, and it was sexy as hell. I had flown both the T-37 and T-38 when I went through pilot training so I was familiar with both. Only the T-38 would do. I placed my application and was soon accepted into the Air Training Command as a T-38 Instructor Pilot. My base of choice was Williams AFB, Arizona, near Phoenix. I got the airplane but not the base. I'd be going to Craig AFB, Alabama, near Selma. Even though I didn't get Williams, I was still happy overall. After living in North Carolina, I could speak Southern.

My wife and I both looked forward to this new opportunity but it was difficult for us to leave Pope. I loved the people, the airplane, and the travel. We spent several days saying our goodbyes. We made lifelong friends at Pope but now we looked forward to meeting new ones in Alabama.

I never saw Irv or Col. Benny again but I did follow their careers. Benny continued his upward climb. He left our squadron to become a Wing Commander at Little Rock in charge of three squadrons. On a low-level training mission one night, an aircraft in a three-ship formation clipped a tree with its wingtip. The aircraft landed successfully with only minor structural damage. Benny was not flying that night. Since it was one of his pilots who was flying, Benny was fired. He was transferred to Rhein-Main where he stayed until his retirement. After his retirement, he ran the "Stars and Stripes" bookstore at the Frankfurt airport. Benny died in 2007 having fought Alzheimer's disease, heart disease and colon cancer.

Irv stayed in the C-130. Apparently he never calmed down. Irv had moved to a nice house in a lake community near Pope. He was having one of his wild squadron parties on a sunny Sunday afternoon. One of Irv's co pilots was a member of the Aero Club at nearby Simmons Army Airfield. Aero Club members could rent airplanes from the club at cost. Their only extra cost was the fuel used. This young man decided he would rent an airplane and put on an airshow for the partygoers. After performing a couple of low passes, he pulled up to set up for another one. He yanked and banked a little too much and it resulted in a hammerhead stall. He wound up with the airplane pointing straight up and out of airspeed. Then the plane nosed straight over into the lake, killing the pilot in front of his horrified wife and young son.

The story of Irv remains unfinished. I was unable to find out where he wound up, but I'm sure it was interesting.

Chapter 2

Selma, Alabama wasn't anything like I had imagined it would be. We only knew it from what we had seen on the nightly news. The place was supposedly a hotbed of racial tension as evidenced by the famous marches from Selma to Montgomery.

Thousands of blacks from all over the U.S. had come to march in solidarity with local citizens who were trying to achieve the right to vote. The first march occurred on Sunday, March 7, 1965, with only 600 participants. The police attacked the marchers with Billy clubs and tear gas. Two days later they attempted a second march but police forced the 2500 protestors back after they had crossed the Edmund Pettus Bridge. U.S. Army soldiers, Alabama National Guardsmen, FBI agents, and Federal Marshalls protected the third march that finally made it to Montgomery. These marches were instrumental to the passage of President Johnson's Voting Rights Act of 1965.

The Selma we discovered in August of 1973 was quiet and boring. No marches, no fighting in the streets, no sit-ins at lunch counters. It was just a slow-paced southern town where everyone, regardless of color, was friendly and respectful to each other.

Doreen and I had a choice. We could live on base and forego our housing allowance, or buy something in town and get a housing supplement added into my pay. Base housing was very unattractive and we wanted to be exposed to the local culture. Living on the base meant we would only interact with fellow Air Force officers and their families. Like Jerry Seinfeld would say, "Not that there's anything wrong with that." We were just looking to widen our circle.

We started looking at houses in downtown Selma. Selma was only five miles from the base and housing was very reasonable. We bought an old Victorian house on King Street. It had 14-foot ceilings, a new kitchen, three bedrooms and a nice back yard for our daughter, Krista, to play in. All this for only $25,000.

The place needed some paint and minor repairs but it was ours, the first house we had ever bought. We quickly got to know our next-door neighbors, Joe and Betty Williams. Joe and Betty were an older couple in their 60's. They were lifelong Selma residents and they filled us in on all the local happenings. Across the street lived Millie and Steve, about our age, with a daughter just a year older than Krista.

This was a working class neighborhood. The houses were built in the late 1940's to early 1950's. They were all single-family homes. All parking was either on the street or on a pad in the back yard. The Alabama River wound its way just south of town and then snakelike, to the south and west through Dallas County.

Chapter 3

I was assigned to the 52nd Flying Training Squadron (FTS). The 52nd FTS was part of the 29th Flying Training Wing at Craig. The Wing consisted of the T-37 section, the T-38s and all maintenance and support functions. I was raring to get to work but I couldn't do anything until I was trained. T-38 Pilot Instructor Training (PIT) School was located at Randolph AFB, Texas. Slots in this program were limited and I had to wait for an opening. The wait could be as long as four months but after a month on the list, a slot opened up due to a cancellation. One of the other candidates was thrown from a horse and broke his leg. One man's misfortune was another's opportunity. A week later, I left for Texas.

USAF Pilot Instructor Training was an intense eight-week course covering all phases of flight training. The T-37 and T-38 student pilot training programs were similar in content. Both consisted of three phases that began with instrument procedures, or how to fly the airplane on the gauges. Then came the contact phase, which concentrated on takeoffs, landings and aerial maneuvers. The third phase was formation: two, three, and four ship.

Our training syllabus for the T-38 instructor course followed the three phases. Relearning to fly the airplane was a joy. The key to flying this or any airplane was to stay ahead of it mentally. The faster the airplane, the further ahead you had to be. The T-38 entered the visual overhead-landing pattern at 300 knots. If you hadn't planned your pitchout, final turn, touchdown and rollout, you were behind the airplane and may be forced to go around; all due to poor planning.

I quickly re-acclimated to the plane and was soon comfortable with the much faster pace. The difficult part was factoring instruction into flying. It wasn't good enough to simply stay ahead of the airplane. I had to learn how to tell a student what we were going to do, then demonstrate it, and then have him repeat it. All this had to be done while zipping along at 400 knots. Sometimes my most carefully crafted instructor spiel on a particular maneuver would just disappear as I struggled to keep the plane in its assigned area. Flying areas were assigned to specific flights. These areas were based on defined radials and distances from navigational aides. These areas were pie-shaped, usually 25 to 30 miles wide and 10,000 feet thick, meaning we flew between 10,000 to 20,000 feet.

There were specified departure and arrival tracks and strict control of area assignments. The procedures were in place to keep airplanes separated, but the ultimate responsibility for separation rested with the pilot. In addition to instructing, flying, and staying ahead of the airplane, I had to keep my head on a swivel looking for traffic conflicts. I remember several training rides at Randolph in which my carefully constructed dialogue abruptly halted as we started to bust out of our area. When this happened I had to calmly regroup and start over from the beginning. This was a humbling experience but it happened to all instructor trainees and I didn't let it affect my attitude.

Chapter 4

The T-38 has front and rear seating, known as tandem seating. The student usually sits in the front with the instructor in the back. The only exception to this was instrument training. During this phase, the student sat in the back, under a hooded canopy. This hood was a canvas covering that ran the length of the canopy. Pulled forward, it blocked out the outside world forcing the student to fly using only the instrument panel. When not in use, the hood could be moved back behind the ejection seat.

My usual seat was in the back. I liked it back there. I sat up a little higher than the front seater and had a clear view of everything, with one exception. In the normal landing attitude, with the wing flaps down, I could see the runway over the head of the front seater. When practicing no flap approaches, while simulating a flap failure, the nose of the airplane was much higher, making it hard to see the runway. The only way to stay aligned was to shift my view from left to right, constantly making small adjustments to stay on the centerline. This ability to land the airplane by looking out the side would prove invaluable later in my career.

Instructor candidates came from varied backgrounds. We all agreed that the most challenging flying was in formation. Formation flying is a counter-intuitive exercise. During your flying career you do all you can to avoid hitting other airplanes. The object in formation flying is to get very close to the lead aircraft - three feet - and stay there until told otherwise. The correct position is an extended line off the leader's leading wing edge. If you draw that line out, your proper position as wingman results in a three-foot separation between the planes. Number two can be either on the left or right, depending on the lead's choice. Your job as number two is to stay in position and help the leader clear the area. The leader communicates with air traffic control for both aircraft. The wingman acknowledges by saying his position. In this case, the response would be "two."

For example, air traffic control issues a radio frequency change:

"Gin 21 Flight, contact Houston Center on 271.3"

Lead responds: "Roger, Gin 21 Flight go 271.3"

Two responds: "Two"

There are several visual signals used in formation as well. A quick pulse of the stick to the left, for example, will dip and then re-level the wing. This is number two's signal to move from the right wing position to the left wing. Number two would crack back on the throttles, move back and slightly down to a position behind lead with sufficient nose to tail clearance; then power back to stop rearward motion, slide to the left and move up and in on the left wing.

Radio frequency changes and fuel states can also be communicated with hand signals. If the two aircraft need to talk about something (maintenance issue, for example), the formation will switch to a discreet frequency where they can talk openly about an issue.

While at Pilot Instructor Training (PIT), it took some work to get my formation flying skills back. The initial tendency is to get into proper position but very gradually slide back to a safer position. I had to fight myself to stay in position. Added to that was learning how to give instructions while flying. I was supposed to be telling a student how I was doing all this and then effectively demonstrating it. On my first few formation rides I did a great impression of Silent Bob. My words wouldn't come. All of my energies were directed at keeping that wingtip in the star, which is what I saw when in proper position. Once I became comfortable flying so close to another airplane again, I regained the power of speech.

Now that my positioning was under control, we moved on to more difficult maneuvers. From flying straight and level, we progressed to turns, climbs and descents. Then on to increasing "G" turns, climbs and descents. My instructor demonstrated the first high G turning descent. It was very smooth and we stayed right in position as he told me what he was doing to maintain such a rock solid platform. Now it was my turn. As soon as the leader started loading up the backpressure on the stick and increasing the G's, things started happening to my airplane. It started bobbing up and down and weaving left and right as I tried to ease on the correct backpressure and bank to stay in position. I was all over the place, except in the right position.

My instructor took the airplane, put us back in position, and we tried it again with the same result. We took a break to talk about it. He gave me a tip that brought it all together for me. The T-38, unlike most airplanes, can be flown flat-footed. The thrust was symmetrical and on centerline so you could fly with your feet off the rudder pedals and flat on the floor. You only really needed to use the rudder pedals for takeoff, in a single engine situation, or when using the brakes. Pushing the bottom of the pedals moved the rudder. Stepping on the top of the pedals activated the brakes. My gyrations in formation occurred because I was flying "free armed." I was moving the control stick with my whole arm and these large stick inputs were causing the plane to hop around like a bug on a hot griddle. My instructor told me to plant my right forearm just behind my right knee, and keep everything from my wrist to my shoulder absolutely still. The only stick input now was from my hand. He also changed my grip on the stick. I went from a death grip to a light touch. From that point on I had no trouble staying in on those five G turns. Now I was having fun.

We moved on to the advanced formation maneuvers starting with pitchouts and rejoins.

These maneuvers are done to give the pilot practice in getting back in position after becoming separated. There are two types of rejoins: turning and straight-ahead. Both maneuvers start the same way, in level flight. The leader signals for a pitchout by pointing his index finger straight up and making a circle with his fingertip. Number two acknowledges with a head nod. The leader goes into a level 45-degree banked turn away from his wingman. The "away" part is important because students in the lead would occasionally turn into you, so you had to be ready for that. As soon as lead turned, or "pitched out," number two started counting to four while remaining level. When he got to "four" he turned after the lead and tried to find him. This may seem like a minor point, but if you couldn't see the lead, the rejoin was off. The T-38 is a very narrow airplane and trying to spot one from a mile or two back is not automatic. All you could see from that far back were the tailpipes and maybe the vertical stabilizer. On a clear day this was not a problem. On a cloudy day you had to work for it. If you couldn't see the lead, you'd ask him to rock his wings. This usually did the trick. If the lead wanted a straight-ahead rejoin he called it on the radio: "Gin 21 Flight, Straight ahead, left side, 280." This meant he wanted you to join on his left wing at 280 knots. Your job as wingman was to get back in position as soon as possible. To do that you needed an airspeed advantage. The lead would be holding his called speed. Normally, a 40 or 50-knot airspeed advantage worked well for a speedy rejoin. Timing was critical, however. As the lead aircraft got bigger in your windscreen you had to control the thrust so as to arrive in position matching his airspeed exactly. Sometimes, bringing the throttles back wouldn't dissipate your energy enough and you sailed right on by the leader. Your ace-in-the-hole were the speed brakes. These were small, rectangular panels normally flush with the bottom of the fuselage. Hydraulically operated, they popped out and slowed the airplane.

The other, more challenging rejoin was the turning rejoin. The leader, after pitching out, would turn at least 180 degrees, wait four seconds, then rock his wings and settle into a left or right 45-degree bank level turn. No radio call is necessary. When you see your lead in a turn, it's a turning rejoin. Your job as two is still to get back in position. But now you must use cutoff angle instead of only airspeed. The term "cutoff angle" is another way of saying, "turn inside of lead." Number two would turn inside of lead until reaching the proper rejoin line. Then it became a matter of flying up this line into position. This maneuver took a lot of practice with occasional scary results. The cutoff angle had to be just right. Too much cutoff and you would pass in front of, or even through the lead. Not enough cutoff and you'd never get there. If done correctly, number two would slide up that extended "wingtip in the star" position with just enough of an airspeed advantage to pull in three feet out and stop. Judging your energy dissipation as you moved in was essential. At the start of the rejoin, lead's aircraft looked small in your windscreen. As you moved up the line using cutoff, he got bigger but his position in the windscreen didn't move. This could be both good and bad. Manage your energy properly and you slid into position. Come in too fast with no correction, you'd go right through him. As my experience increased I did learn one trick to managing too much energy while trying the turning rejoin. If I had too much energy as I was sliding up the line, I would start a barrel roll about 20 feet from lead and do a complete turn around his aircraft. By the end of the roll I was back in proper position. The roll had dissipated the excess energy.

The normal return to base ended with a pitchout over the end of the runway. The formation then landed single ship. As we advanced in training, we began to practice formation landings. The leader would set up a long, straight-in approach. He would configure with gear and flaps and fly down the glide slope to the runway. Number two would maintain position and mirror the leader, configuring with him. Number two would then have to "keep the faith." Number two had to trust the lead and stay in his slot. If you did that, you would come down and land without ever having seen the runway; faith, indeed.

The next phase of training moved us from two ship to four ship. All of the basics of two ship still applied but four ship required more planning for lead. Lead was responsible for staying in the area so he had to allow for the two extra airplanes. Four ship rejoins required a much larger area to complete than a two ship rejoin.

The term for proper formation position was called "fingertip." Looking down at your left hand, palm down, the middle finger is the leader, two is on the right, three and four are on the left (the thumb doesn't participate).

A two-ship mission started with both airplanes taking the runway, and then lining up in an extended fingertip position. Number two was still lined up, wingtip in the star, but separated by 25 feet, instead of three feet. The lead gave the run-up signal and both airplanes advanced throttles to 100%. Lead tapped his helmet and gave an exaggerated head nod then released his brakes and selected minimum afterburner. Afterburner was a throttle bump above 100 percent. It kicked in extra thrust by mixing fuel with the engine exhaust and reigniting the mix. This was really spectacular at night when twin blue flames shot ten feet out of the tail pipes.

Number two selected maximum afterburner, then adjusted as necessary to stay in position. Two mirrored the lead for gear and flaps, and then slid into position three feet out.

The four-ship takeoff had a few differences. The lead had to leave enough room for three and four when taking the runway. If lead took the left side, three would take the right so that four would already be in position when three joined on the leader's left wing on departure. As lead and two rolled down the runway, three gave the run-up signal to four. When lead and two broke ground, three nodded, released brakes and went into afterburner. Four just followed along, configured when three did, and then slid into position.

The Pilot Instructor program exposed us to the common student errors. Our Instructors, playing the part of students, attempted to wander out of the assigned flying areas. They entered a loop at 400 knots instead of the specified 500 knots. Back in the traffic pattern, they "forgot" to lower the gear prior to the final turn. They overshot the runway or attempted to land from a too steep approach. In short, they flew like typical students and wanted us to correct their mistakes. We couldn't simply point out the errors. We had to analyze why it happened and propose corrective action. Sometimes this meant taking control of the airplane. Other times just an appropriate comment would suffice. The risk factor was especially high in formation. When your wingman is only three feet away and you're doing 400 knots, reaction time is minimal.

One of the scenarios our instructors drilled into us was the unexpected student maneuver. A typical one follows: your wingman is on your right side and you set up for a pitchout and rejoin. Your student gives the pitchout signal but then attempts to turn into the wingman instead of away. If allowed to happen, this is disastrous for both airplanes. The instructor must anticipate by watching and listening to the student. From the moment they enter pilot training, students are constantly reminded to "clear" the area. This means turn and look where you're going prior to turning the airplane into that space. As I watched my instructor, who was playing a student, I noticed he cleared to the right even though he'd be turning left. Because of this I tightly guarded the stick ready to take corrective action and, sure enough, he tried to turn into the wingman. Because I watched and anticipated, I prevented a mid-air collision. We were taught never to push the safety envelope but we had to let the students go far enough in order for them to learn. If we were too overprotective no progress would ever be made.

I felt very confidant and well trained by the time I graduated from PIT in January of 1974. Now it was time to go back to Alabama to face some real students.

Chapter 5

Undergraduate Pilot Training (UPT) is a yearlong program that trains new officers how to fly jets.

Prior to beginning the primary, or T-37 phase, all applicants had to prove themselves through a 30-hour flight program in the Cessna 172. The Cessna program was staffed with civilian instructors. The purpose of this program was similar to the ROTC flight program I completed in college. It weeded out candidates who didn't have those qualities the Air Force deemed essential to becoming a successful pilot. This was a very cost effective way to eliminate the most obvious non-starter candidates. Students who were consistently airsick or just plain scared were quickly eliminated; the same for the uncoordinated or those who cracked under pressure. But just getting through the Cessna program was no guarantee that you would be able to go all the way and get your wings. About 1/3 of all candidates were eliminated over the course of a year, most of them in the T-37 phase. The T-37 was a short, squat, two-engine jet with side-by-side seating. The engines produced a loud, high-pitched whine. The airplane was known as the "Tweet" or the "Dog Whistle."

The students in our program were an elite bunch. All were college graduates and some were graduates of the service academies. All met strict selection criteria and were highly motivated. When our students reached the T-38 phase they had accumulated about 120 flying hours, 90 in a low-performance jet (T-37), and 30 in the Cessna program. Now we were to take these students with low experience and pair them with a high performance aircraft.

My squadron, the 52nd Flying Training Squadron, had four different flights (student groups): "F," "G," "H" and "I." There was also a Standardization/Evaluation section. This group administered check rides to the instructors. A separate Check Section gave check rides to the students. The T-38 training phase lasted six months. The four Flights or groups ran the gamut of training. "F" flight, for example, would be in the beginner, or instrument phase. "I" flight, ready to graduate, was in the four ship formation phase.

I had been assigned to "H" flight and they had just begun the formation phase when I arrived. The students each had three or four rides and had not soloed in formation yet. Soloing in formation was a major accomplishment in the T-38 program; second in importance only to the initial solo in the contact phase.

Captain Doug Collert was our Flight Commander. My fellow line instructors were: Lt Greg Barrett, Lt Rob O'Connell, Lt Cal James, and Captain Stan Sparks. All the instructors, except Stan, were FAIPs. This was Air Force speak for "First Assignment Instructor Pilots." This was their first assignment after graduating pilot training. Stan, like me, had come from a previous aircraft.

He was a C-141 pilot. He had done a lot of traveling in the 141 and he wanted to stay put with his family for a few years. All the IPs had three students assigned to them but since I was coming into their program late, I got to share two students, one from Stan and one from Greg.

Chapter 6

My first ride with a real student was a formation ride. I was paired up with Greg and two of his students. These students were both good but with only three formation rides each, were not that comfortable in formation. I started out as lead. We followed a standard profile for this phase including: takeoff, departure, normal maneuvering in fingertip, pitchouts and rejoins, area departure, traffic pattern entry, followed by single ship landings. Since I hadn't flown with this student before, I would demonstrate the first maneuver, and then let him try it. We flew half the ride as lead, then swapped positions with Greg and took the wing. Some of those "what if" scenarios in PIT came true on my first ride with an actual student. This student was a former navigator with the rank of Captain. I think he may have been nervous because he hadn't flown with me before. Flying with a fellow Captain may have spooked him since his regular instructor was a First Lieutenant. Whatever the reason, his flying suffered because of it.

He made several of the classic errors I had been warned about. Once we got into our flying area, I gave him control of the airplane and told him to set up for a straight-ahead rejoin. By the time he set up the maneuver we were heading out of our area into the adjacent one. I took the airplane back, got us back into our area, and set up for the pitchout and rejoin. When this was done, I gave him back the airplane and the go-ahead to do the maneuver. Our wingman was on our right. My student looked at the wingman, gave the signal, and then cleared right. I knew what was coming. He attempted to turn the wrong way right into our wingman. I was ready for him, however. As soon as I felt the first input on the stick I took over and rolled left. I asked him why he was trying to kill us but he couldn't answer.

We did a couple of pitchout/rejoins each then we practiced some G loaded wing work. We instructors constantly pushed the students to improve. A simple way to do this in formation was through G loading. Normal straight and level flying resulted in 1 G (force of gravity). A 60-degree bank level turn produced 2 Gs. A 500-knot loop started out at 5 or 6 Gs. These high G maneuvers pushed your blood supply from your head into your core and legs. To counter this, we wore G-suits, which were inflatable chaps-like devices worn around the mid section and legs which responded to G forces by filling with air. The G-suit would squeeze the legs and stomach and keep the blood supply from moving downward. Without restricting the blood flow, a high G maneuver could cause a blackout; not a good result in a high-speed airplane.

Greg and I let the students fly and they were staying in position but they weren't pushing their limits. It was our turn. Within a few minutes we were doing four and five G turns around cumulus clouds. In this kind of workout, we were all breathing hard and sweating. About 15 minutes of this back and forth was enough and we gave the airplanes back to the students and they practiced for a while.

My student finally relaxed enough to fly up to his potential and I learned a valuable lesson that day. Some students can be easily intimidated so it was important for me to put them at ease before we flew. To the student, the instructor was a powerful figure that could crush your dreams of a flying career so it was important for the student to trust and not fear the instructor. Only by being relaxed and at ease could the student perform up to his potential. This approach to instructor-student relationships was starkly different from the prevailing attitude when I went through pilot training. Back then, the operative words for the instructors' treatment of students were: fear, sarcasm and ridicule. Things were certainly changing for the better.

Chapter 7

The instrument phase was the start of the T-38 program. Before we even began this phase we gave the students a freebie. It was called a "Dollar Ride" because the student would give their instructors a dollar for the privilege of the first T-38 ride. The money went into a kitty to fund squadron parties. Prior to this first ride the students had been to ground school and learned all about the airplane. They were required to master all the systems, learn the limitations and the emergency procedures. After completing ground school, they were given a simulator ride to familiarize them with the cockpit layout. The Dollar Ride was fun for both the student and the instructor. They got to see the capabilities of the aircraft and we got to show off a bit. Part of the ride included a supersonic run. None of the students had ever broken the sound barrier before, but after this ride they were members of the Mach 1+ Club.

Most of the students did well in the instrument phase. They would preview the aircraft lesson in the simulator so there were no surprises. If they had problems in the simulator, they would try it again until they got it right. They also had experience flying on instruments from the T-37 phase. The T-38 had different instrumentation but they at least knew how to build their scan, or instrument crosscheck. Once the student mastered the lesson on the simulator, they would then try it in the airplane.

Flying on instruments in any airplane required building a "scan" for that particular plane. Building this scan meant locating which instruments to crosscheck in order to keep the airplane where you wanted it. A proper crosscheck or scan centered on one main instrument, usually the Attitude Director Indicator or ADI, with quick systematic looks to the other gauges. A typical scan would start with the ADI, then a glance at the airspeed gauge, back to the ADI, to the vertical velocity gauge, to the heading or course, then back to the ADI. The scan had to be systematic and it had to keep moving. The purpose of this back and forth was to see trends and correct them on the ADI. If you spotted a gradual climb while you were supposed to be level then a change had to be made on the ADI. If you stopped too long on one of the gauges, bad things usually followed. Concentrating on the airspeed could mean an unintended climb or descent. Watching just the heading could jeopardize your speed control.

Chapter 8

The flight line routine was split into morning and afternoon sessions, and the groups would alternate. "H" flight, for example, would be on mornings this week and on afternoons next week. The morning sessions started at 6:00 a.m. and went to 1:00 p.m. The afternoon sessions started at noon and went to 7:00 p.m. The only exception to this schedule was when we practiced night flying.

Every flying day was structured the same way. The day began with a weather briefing and student quizzing. Students would be called at random to stand up and recite the steps required for certain emergency procedures. The students had to know these cold, without hesitation or omission. If they forgot a step, or got the wording wrong or hesitated, they wouldn't fly that day. After the emergency procedures quiz was completed, individual flight briefings started. An instructor and his students occupied a table. When the instructor briefed a student, the rest of his students would listen in.

Students sat in the rear cockpit, under the hood, for instrument rides. The rides began with basic maneuvers like maintaining straight and level flight. Speed variations would be added. Once a skill was mastered, a new task was added. Turns were introduced, then climbing and descending turns, then speed changes during turns and so on. Mastering these individual skills was building the student toward the ultimate goal of instrument flight: flying instrument approaches through the weather to a safe landing. At the end of the instrument phase, the student would be able to safely fly every type of instrument approach available in the T-38. Once the student passed his instrument phase check ride, he would move on to the contact phase.

The contact phase was make-or-break time for most students. The key elements of this phase were takeoffs and landings. Other topics covered in this phase were: taxiing, departure, climb, area entry, aerobatics, radio procedures, area departure, traffic pattern entry, single-engine and no-flap landings, checklist usage and ramp procedures (how to get in and out of a parking spot). If the student progressed normally, he would be eligible to solo after six to eight rides. T-38 solo was a major milestone. 95% of students who soloed would go on to successfully complete the program. The other 5% would stumble on the formation phase.

For these first few contact rides the students were behind the airplane. We would be entering the area for maneuvers and they would still be thinking about the takeoff but gradually they would catch up. Our goal was to get them planning their maneuvers ahead of the airplane. One of the reasons why this was so important was fuel usage. The average contact mission lasted about an hour and fifteen minutes. The student had to be able to get to his assigned area, sequence his maneuvers and figure out when to leave the area so he could arrive back in the traffic pattern and practice a few landings. After all this he had to arrive back on the ramp with a safe amount of fuel.

Chapter 9

At civilian airports, the tower controls traffic. At student pilot training bases, the Runway Supervisory Unit (RSU) controlled the traffic. The RSU was a small trailer-like structure on stilts that was situated along the side of the runway about 1500 feet from the approach end. It was fully air-conditioned and radio equipped. It also had hard-wired phone lines installed and flare gun ports for emergencies. An Instructor Pilot (IP) and three students manned the RSU. IPs wishing to be controllers underwent a rigorous six–week training program before being allowed to direct traffic. One student acted as a recorder writing down takeoff and landing times as well as controller comments. A second student, a spotter, acted as the eyes of the unit. He faced the approach end of the runway using binoculars to call the oncoming aircraft configuration for the controller. This spotter assured the controller that all approaching aircraft had landing gear, flaps and lights in the proper position. The third student faced the departure end of the runway. He would warn the controller of any impending conflicts on his end of the runway.

The controller acted like a maestro. He would safely sequence all the airplanes in the pattern. He had to know where every aircraft was all the time. The maximum number of airplanes allowed in the pattern was twelve. These twelve included dual ships (instructor and student aboard), solos, and formation flights. Radio calls were used to keep everyone aware of each other's position. A call had to be made when entering the pattern from the area, when entering initial, pitching out, the final turn, go-around and requesting a closed pattern (a short cut allowing you to by-pass the outside downwind). Everyone had to call, and to make the system work properly, everyone had to listen-up. Only by listening could you know where everyone else was.

Some problems arose when aircraft would cut off each other's radio transmissions. Sometimes the students would forget their call sign or just get so zoned in on landing the airplane that they weren't listening. This is where the flares came in. On more than one occasion, a student tried to land gear up and I had to fire a flare because he was not acknowledging my instructions on the radio.

Back in the mid 1970's we trained quite a few Saudi and Iranian student pilots. Some of them were very good but several were really bad. These students came from very wealthy, even royal families. Language was just one of the barriers they faced. Their major hurdle was the technology gap. They were at a tremendous disadvantage compared to their American classmates. Growing up in Saudi Arabia or Iran did not prepare them well for the high-tech world of jets. These students were under the ultimate pressure to succeed. If they washed out, they would be returned to their homes and were rumored to be executed for their failure. Their high motivation didn't always lead to graduation.

Most had a good understanding of English but throw in the jargon of flight school and things started to crumble. Their ability to speak and understand English was inversely proportional to the amount of stress in a given situation. I had taken one of my Iranian students, Ahmed, on a cross-country flight. Our destination was Ellington AFB in Houston one Friday afternoon in June. The weather was not that bad but there were several thunderstorms along our route of flight. The thunderstorms were generating a lot of lightning and turbulence.

I was sitting in the rear cockpit and Ahmed in the front. We saw three or four large lightning strikes off our left wing and I could tell Ahmed was getting antsy. Despite my reassurances about our safety, I could hear Ahmed muttering to himself in Farsi. When the next lightning bolt flashed, Ahmed unstrapped from his ejection seat, turned around and kneeled down on the seat facing backwards. He then began to pray. I was dumbfounded, and busy. When Ahmed decided to take his prayer break, he had been flying. Since he was no longer in a position to fly the airplane, I took over and tried to figure out what this crazy bastard was up to. He was praying because he thought he was going to die, regardless of what I told him. I guess the stress brought on by the weather shut down his ability to understand English. Once we cleared the line of thunderstorms, he stopped praying, strapped himself back in, and soon sounded like his old self.

After we landed we had a long discussion about weather, aircraft control and basic safety (not unstrapping in flight). He seemed to understand what I was telling him. Eventually Ahmed washed out of the program. He couldn't fly in formation so he was sent back to Iran and was never heard from again.

The most important part of the contact training phase was the traffic pattern, which included takeoffs and landings. The traffic pattern consisted of specific points that all planes had to navigate over. Aircraft leaving the pattern had to follow a specific ground track. The same was true for entering the pattern. Everyone operated on the same radio frequency and called when reaching key points in the pattern. By listening, a pilot in the pattern knew where the other aircraft were. The RSU controller had the big picture. The controller issued landing clearances or go-around instructions. The ultimate responsibility for separation from other aircraft lay with the pilot. In the traffic pattern, you always kept your head moving around and your ears open. The RSU controller paid special attention to the solo students. As a controller, I knew the dual aircraft would usually do the right thing but I watched the solos and waited for them to do the wrong thing. The solos could get in trouble in any number of ways. The majority of the solo students did a fantastic job and flew without incident. It was the exceptions that warranted close scrutiny. They occasionally forgot to configure the airplane prior to the final turn, even though "gear check" was a mandatory radio call in the turn.

They would get so focused on traffic spacing, turning at the right time, or listening to the radios that they neglected to lower the gear handle and/or flaps for landing. My response was always the same: "Go Around." So they went around and set up for another landing. The landing itself was another critical time for the solo student. The T-38 would land in a normal, nose-high attitude. This attitude was established on final approach and held all the way down to the runway while gradually decreasing power. If the student had the airplane too high off the ground, the nose kept coming up while the airspeed decreased, a dangerous situation. When I saw this developing, I would send the student around. The proper response from the student would be to lower the nose by relaxing backpressure on the stick and advancing the power to maximum. This would get the airplane accelerating again and kept it from stalling. On rare occasions, the student would attempt to keep the aircraft from touching the ground by keeping backpressure on the stick while simultaneously pushing the power to maximum. The result of this unhealthy combination was called a saber dance. During a saber dance, the airplane remains nose-high as it walks itself down the runway, swaying left and right. The airplane can't accelerate because the pilot is holding too much backpressure on the stick. If held too long, the airplane will crash, so it's very critical to lower the nose by relaxing backpressure

Since the maximum number of planes in the pattern was twelve, there were times when several solo students would be in the pattern together. One of our training bases was Webb AFB, Texas. One fateful day at Webb, the pattern was full, twelve aircraft. Four of these twelve were solos. Two of the solos were Iranian students. The following event demonstrates how high pressure and language barriers can combine to cause big problems. Iranian student #1 was in the final turn, gear and flaps down, all is well. Iranian student #2 was on outside downwind. Student #1 was cleared for a touch and go and he safely landed. On his go around after the landing, a long tongue of flame shot out the tail of number 2 engine. The RSU student observer called out the problem to the controller who turned and verified the fire. The controller, for whatever reason, couldn't think of the call sign of the distressed airplane. The number of solos in the pattern may have confused the controller, but he did know that the student in the fiery aircraft was an Iranian. Knowing this, the controller said: "Iranian student in the T-38 pattern at Webb, you're on fire, eject." At which point, both Iranian students in the pattern at Webb ejected, one from the stricken airplane and one from a perfectly good airplane. Both students parachuted safely to the ground. Both aircraft were total losses.

My off time schedule was a full one. One of the perks of the job was being able to come home every night. My daughter Krista was four when our son Jason was born in December of 1974. Spending as much time with them was my first priority. The realities of an Air Force career cut into the family time, however. Competition among Officers was very keen and we were encouraged to do whatever we could to distinguish ourselves from our contemporaries.

There were university extension courses available at night on the base. Master's degree programs for both business and counseling were available. I enrolled in the counseling program and obtained my Master's degree in Counseling and Guidance within two years. I also completed the Air Force Air Command and Staff College course by correspondence. Neither of these made me a better pilot but the Air Force believed it would some day make me a better administrator. My sole desire was to fly but the Air Force had a different plan. I was willing to go along with this theory as long as I could keep flying and it didn't force me behind a desk.

Chapter 10

The third leg of the student-flying curriculum was formation. This was my personal favorite and I didn't try to hide my enthusiasm from my students. Some of the students were afraid of formation. It required total concentration and coordination. As tense as it may sound, to do it well, you had to relax. The harder you gripped that stick, the rougher you flew. Formation flying required the student to learn both lead and wing positions. The lead had to plan his maneuvers well in advance. He could no longer think for himself; he had to plan for two, three, or four airplanes. Staying in the assigned area took some planning. This was an easy task for one airplane. But could get a lot more complicated when three more aircraft were added to the formation. When leading a four-ship, it was lead's responsibility to keep all his airplanes in the area. Situational awareness was a key factor in the leader's planning.

Lead also did the clearing for his formation ensuring the airspace you were about to enter was safe. Before the flight, the lead briefed the mission. He listed the maneuvers and their sequence and also set a "bingo" fuel. This was a "return to base" fuel. Regardless of what had been accomplished on the ride, when a formation member declared "bingo," the formation started back. Halfway into the ride, the lead would change, and the maneuvers would be repeated with a new leader.

This switch ensured that students got to practice both positions.

The formation phase put pressure on the students. If they could solo in formation, they knew they would finish the program and get their wings. As instructors, we knew that we would lose a few more students before this phase was over. Our students were nervous but we did our best to put them at ease. We also did our best to hide our apprehension from them. It was one thing to fly three feet away from another airplane at 400 knots, that wasn't a problem. The leap of faith came when we had to hand the airplane over to the student and let him try it. Our hands were never far from the controls. The goal of this training was to get the students proficient enough to solo in formation. At the end of each phase of training: instrument, contact, and now formation, the student had to pass a check ride. These were all high-pressure rides but the solo formation ride was THE ride. Once the student soloed in formation, he was assured of getting his wings.

When there were only a few rides left until graduation, we were able to have a little fun with the students. A typical four-ship consisted of two dual ships and two solos. One of the maneuvers practiced was a pitchout and straight ahead rejoin. After the pitchout, lead would call out which side #2 was to join and what speed to join at. Rejoin speed was normally 280 to 300 knots. We instructors could have a little fun with our students by agreeing prior to takeoff that we would rejoin at 250 knots instead of the called speed, 300 knots. Lead would pitch out; make the radio call and wait. #2, the other dual ship, rejoined at 250 knots. Then we both would watch as #3 and #4 flashed by our position with 50 knots of overtake. It was safe, but it was funny.

After instructing for 18 months I was appointed the Chief of Check Section. There were six of the most experienced instructors in Check Section so it was an honor for me to take this position. Our task was to administer all student check rides for all three phases of the program. Because of my position, I frequently had to fly with students who were candidates for elimination from the program. One such student was Marvin.

Marvin was quiet, polite and very intense. He had trouble getting through each phase but each time he had passed his final ride in both the instrument and contact phase. His problem wasn't so much his hand-eye coordination in formation, but his lack of judgment. This was a major factor in grading our student pilots. We were teaching them the skills to fly but throughout the year we stressed the proper use of judgment. Not only did we show them how to land the airplane, we also showed them the danger of trying to save a landing from an unstable approach. A situation like this required good judgment. Marvin could fly in formation but he had trouble in recognizing a hazardous situation as it developed.

Marvin was down to his last ride, his elimination ride. If he failed this ride he was on his way back to Louisiana without his wings. Marvin and I would fly together. In the other airplane was my good Bud and fellow instructor Greg Barrett. Greg was flying with his student, Bob Johnson, who was progressing normally. We all sat down and briefed the flight. Marvin and I would lead off, perform a number of maneuvers, then switch lead and repeat. I took the extra time to put Marvin at ease prior to the flight. I told him the more relaxed and less worried he was, the better his performance would be. Marvin was his typical, quiet self. I didn't know if my talk helped. I told Marvin how the flight would be operated. He would be flying as if he were solo. I would do minimal instructing, but I would be observing his flying skills and judgment.

Marvin did a stellar job as lead. He kept us in the area, sequenced his maneuvers well and took care of his wingman. We switched positions and took our spot on the wing. The pitchout and turning rejoin took longer than normal. Marvin seemed hesitant to fly up that extended line into proper position, three feet from lead. With a little encouragement, he slid into position. Marvin got quite a workout as we hung on through several turning climbs and descents.

Now it was time for some close and extended trail. The "trail" position flown by number two is a 60-degree cone flown behind the lead. A "close" trail is from 500 to 1000 feet back; 1000 to 2000 feet back is the "extended" position. The wingman's job is to stay in the cone behind lead regardless of the maneuver being performed. Lead would typically do lazy eights, chandelles, barrel rolls and turn reversals. The wingman uses power and cutoff to remain in the cone behind the leader, keeping him in sight at all times. We did a few simple maneuvers, and then lead started into a barrel roll. Normally it's not hard to stay in position during the barrel roll, but this one was done around the sun. Lead started down and we were right with him. Lead then started pulling and rolling and Marvin started falling out of the cone. In order to get back in the cone, Marvin cut towards the lead but as lead continued the barrel roll, Marvin ended up heading directly into the sun and lead was now gone. Marvin's next move would decide his future (and almost mine as well). When the wingman loses sight of lead, the correct action is to turn away from his last known position. When we last saw lead, he was rolling left in about 90 degrees of bank. Marvin should have rolled right and pulled to avoid a conflict; instead he rolled further left and that's when I took control of the airplane and rolled right, sealing Marvin's fate.

     I almost acted too late. When I next saw lead, I was right side up, in level flight. The lead aircraft flashed by us in a split second. He was upside down and our wings missed each other by a foot. Neither of us had time to say anything on the radio but one of us hit the mike button at that instant and made a sound as we nearly smacked into each other. We headed back to Craig without trying to find each other again. Marvin hadn't said a word. He knew what was coming. Back on the ground I debriefed him for over an hour. He had failed the ride. His flying skills were acceptable. The reason for his elimination was his lack of judgment. By trying to do the opposite of what was called for in that situation he almost cost all four of us our lives along with the loss of both aircraft.

Russian AN-12 pilot and Jim Carter in Calcutta, India, 1971

Gary Powers and the U2

USAF T-38 Trainer

USAF C-130

USAF U-2

U2 pilot suited up for a high flight

Col. Lyman Kidder and Lt. Col. George Freese greet Capt. Jim Carter after his initial U-2 solo flight.

PART III

Chapter 1

The summer of 1977 was its normal self, very hot and humid. Along with the heat came a rumor that Air Training Command was reducing its number of bases. Everyone was on edge. It didn't take long for the rumor to become reality. We received notice in June that Craig would be closing. The Air Force was under congressional pressure to cut its budget and Craig AFB became expendable. This meant that we all had choices to make. Those of us who still had an obligation to Air Training Command could continue flying the T-38 but would have to do it at one of the remaining pilot training bases. My obligation to ATC was fulfilled so I was free to apply for any flying job I wanted.

The base closure was a stroke of good fortune because now I could apply for something I had always wanted, but couldn't until now. My dream-flying job was a single seat, single engine jet. There weren't too many of these jobs left in the Air Force. The U-2 was at the top of my list.

The U-2 is a high altitude, single seat, reconnaissance aircraft. Up to now, it was my unreachable star because I hadn't met the qualifications. One of the requirements for flying the U-2 was having at least 1000 hours of jet time. An additional requirement stated that the applicant had to have aircraft commander experience in at least two different airplanes. My T-38 IP job gave me over 1100 hours of jet time and it was my second aircraft commander job. Now I had the qualifications needed for this dream job.

The U-2 was my top choice but I had other options in case my application was rejected. I could go back to the C-130 or fly the F-15 fighter aircraft. The F-15 was a great airplane but the location would be in Alamogordo, New Mexico, which was terrible. All my hopes were riding on the U-2 since the other options were unattractive.

There were several reasons I wanted into the U-2 program. It met my single engine, single seat criteria. It was the most challenging airplane in the world to fly, I was fascinated by its history, and it had an important mission.

In 1977 the airplane was no longer flying over hostile territory. Through the development of technology and satellite usage we no longer had to fly over dangerous areas. Cameras had been developed that could peer sideways into a country and did so with amazing resolution. The true value of the U-2, that is still true today, is its unpredictability. Bad guys knew when the satellites would be overhead, but they never knew when the U-2 would show up.

Chapter 2

The U-2 was a technical marvel and it played an important role in world political events. The Cold War era was synonymous with the U-2.

The U-2 program started in the early 1950's. The U.S. military wanted to keep an eye on Soviet arms development post World War II. Russia had gone from being an ally during the war to being a threat after the war ended. In the early 1950's the best intelligence we had on the interior of the Soviet Union was from captured German Luftwaffe photos taken during the war. These photos only showed the territory west of the Ural Mountains. This lack of knowledge of Soviet capabilities prompted a call for overflights of Soviet airspace. The Soviet air defenses aggressively attacked all aircraft near its borders. The existing reconnaissance aircraft, primarily bombers converted for reconnaissance duty, were vulnerable to anti-aircraft artillery, missiles and fighters. Richard Leghorn of the U.S. Air Force suggested that an aircraft flying above 65,000 feet should be safe from the MIG-17. The MIG-17 was the Soviet's best interceptor but it could barely reach 45,000 feet. Leghorn and others believed that Soviet radar could not track high altitude reconnaissance aircraft. Leghorn's belief, however, was based on outdated intelligence. Since the war the Soviets had improved their radar technology and were able to track aircraft over 65,000 feet.

The highest-flying airplane in the 50's was the English Canberra, which could reach 48,000 feet. The U.S. version of the Canberra was the B-57. The Americans modified the B-57 with longer, thinner wings, new engines, and a lighter-than-normal airframe, which enabled it to reach 67,000 feet.

U.S. Air Force (USAF) planners reasoned that an aircraft that could fly at 70,000 feet would be safely beyond the reach of Soviet fighters, missiles and radar. In 1953 another USAF officer, John Seaberg, proposed building an aircraft that could reach this height over a target with a 1500 nautical mile operational radius. The USAF decided to only solicit designs from smaller aircraft companies that could give the project the attention it deserved. The USAF gave contracts to Bell Aircraft, Martin Aircraft, and Fairchild to develop proposals for the new reconnaissance aircraft. Officials at Lockheed heard about the project and decided to submit an unsolicited proposal. Lockheed executive, John Carter (not a relative) suggested that the design eliminate landing gear and avoid combat load factor requirements. These two items would save weight and increase altitude.

Lockheed asked Clarence "Kelly" Johnson to come up with such a design. Johnson was Lockheed's best aeronautical engineer. He was responsible for the P-38, the P-80, and the F-104. He was also known for completing projects ahead of schedule. He worked in a separate division of the company called "The Skunk Works." This strange name was originated by one of Johnson's engineers. This team engineer, Irv Culver, was a fan of Al Capp's newspaper comic strip, "Lil Abner" in which there was a running gag about a mysterious and smelly place deep in the forest called the "Skonk Works." There, a strong tonic called Kickapoo Joy Juice, was brewed from skunks, old shoes and other weird ingredients. One day, Culver's phone rang and he answered it by saying "Skonk Works, inside man Culver speaking." Fellow employees quickly adopted the name for their secret division of Lockheed. "Skonk Works" became "Skunk Works" and the once informal nickname is now the registered trademark of the company.

Johnson's design was called the CL-282. Johnson started with an F-104 fuselage. The F-104 Starfighter was basically a big engine with small, fin-like wings, and was affectionately known as the "missile with a man in it," which describes it perfectly. To this dart-like fuselage, Johnson attached long, glider-like wings and used a General Electric J-73 engine to power the airplane. The resultant aircraft was a jet-powered glider. It took off from a dolly, landed on skids, and could reach 70,000 feet with a 2,000-mile range. The USAF rejected Kelly's design in favor of the Bell X-16 and the modified B-57. Their reasons for the rejection were: lack of landing gear, and the use of the GE-73 engine instead of the more proven Pratt and Whitney J-57.

Some high officials in the USAF favored the CL-282 because of its higher potential altitude and smaller radar cross section. These officials recommended the design to the CIA. The CIA looked at the design and told the Intelligence Systems Panel, a civilian group advising the USAF on aerial reconnaissance, about the CL-282. Aspects of its design that the USAF saw as flaws appealed to the panel.

Edwin Land, the father of instant photography, and also a member of the panel, proposed to the CIA that they should fund and operate the aircraft. CIA Director Allen Dulles was reluctant to have the CIA conduct its own overflights. Land told President Eisenhower about the aircraft and Eisenhower agreed with Land that the CIA should operate the aircraft. Dulles finally agreed with the President. Meanwhile Seaburg helped persuade USAF to support the CL-282, but with the higher performance J-57 engine. Final approval for the joint CIA-USAF project came in November 1954. Funding came from the CIA, which used un-vouchered government money.

Lockheed received a $22.5 million contract in March of 1955 for the first 20 aircraft, with the first $1.26 million mailed directly to Johnson's home in February 1955 to keep work going during negotiations. Lockheed agreed to deliver the first aircraft by July and the last one by November 1956. Lockheed delivered at $3.5 million under budget because the aircraft was based on the F-104; only the wings, tail and landing gear were different.

Procurement of the aircraft's components occurred secretly. When Johnson ordered altimeters calibrated to 80,000 feet from a company whose instruments only went to 45,000 feet, the CIA set up a cover story involving experimental rocket aircraft. Shell Oil developed a new low-volatility, low vapor pressure jet fuel that would not evaporate at high altitudes. This fuel became known as JP-7. Due to the commonality of the ingredients in JP-7 and Flit, a Shell insect repellent, manufacturing several thousand gallons of JP-7 for the CL-282 in 1955 caused a nationwide shortage of Flit. Shell had no comment about the cause of the shortage.

The CL-282 was renamed the U-2 in July 1955. The "U" referred to the deliberately vague designation "Utility" instead of "R," the normal designation for reconnaissance aircraft. The U-1 and U-3 already existed, so the U-2 was chosen. The joint CIA-USAF project was called Project Dragon Lady.

The USAF sought to take total control of the project but President Eisenhower was opposed to military personnel flying the aircraft. USAF recruited pilots for the program but they had to resign their military commissions before joining the agency as civilians. The program offered high salaries and the USAF promised that pilots could return to their units at their former ranks when their U-2 duties ended.

On August 1, 1955, the first flight occurred at Groom Lake, a salt flat in Nevada on the north side of Area 51. The test pilot, Tony LeVier, was only supposed to do a high-speed taxi. The wings were so efficient that the aircraft became airborne at 70 knots. On August 8, the aircraft flew on purpose and reached 32,000 feet. By August 16, it reached 52,000 feet, an altitude never before reached in sustained flight. By September 8, it reached 65,000 feet. Testing continued with eight overflights in the United States. By April 1956 the project leaders were convinced that the aircraft was ready for actual deployment.

A committee of Army, Navy, USAF, CIA, NSA, and State Department representatives created lists of priority targets for the aircraft. The U-2 project received the list, drew up flight plans, and the committee provided a detailed rationale for presidential approval.

With approval from the National Advisory Committee on Aeronautics (NACA), the CIA developed a cover story for the U-2 that described the aircraft as a high altitude weather research plane. The cover story would be used if the aircraft were lost over hostile territory. To support the story, U-2s took weather photos that appeared in the press.

Some advisors disagreed with the cover story. They believed that if the U-2 was lost, the U.S. should acknowledge its use as prevention against surprise attacks. This advice was not followed and the weather cover story led to the diplomatic disaster that followed the downing of a U-2 flown by Francis Gary Powers in May of 1960.

President Eisenhower worried that overflights of the Soviet Union might cause a war. While the U-2 was under development, Eisenhower proposed to Khrushchev that the

Soviet Union and the U.S. should grant each other access to airfields to photograph military installations. Khrushchev rejected this "Open Skies" policy. Meanwhile, the CIA told Eisenhower that the Soviets could not track the U-2. The CIA belief was based on old Soviet radar systems, which were not as effective at high altitudes as current Soviet systems. CIA Director Dulles also told Eisenhower that if an aircraft were lost, the pilot would almost certainly not survive. For all of these reasons, Eisenhower approved 10 days of overflights.

The first overflight of hostile territory covered Poland and East Germany in June 1956. The first Soviet overflight was on July 4, 1956. The main target was the Soviet submarine construction program in Leningrad. The next flights overflew both Moscow and Leningrad searching for "Bison" bombers and rocket factories. The U.S. intelligence community feared that the Soviets were outbuilding us in bombers, creating what came to be known as the "Bomber Gap."

The CIA found that the Soviets could not consistently track the U-2s so the Soviets didn't know that Moscow and Leningrad had been overflown. The U-2s' photos showed images of MIG-15s and MIG-17s attempting and failing to intercept the aircraft. This strengthened the CIA's belief that the Soviets could not shoot down a U-2.

The Soviets protested the overflights. The U.S. replied that no American military planes had overflown Soviet territory. The Soviet protest showed that they could track the U-2 for extended periods and this caused Eisenhower to halt the overflights. The eight overflights had already shown that a "Bomber Gap" did not exist, but because the Eisenhower Administration could not disclose the source of its intelligence, congressional and public debate over the supposed bomber gap continued.

In May 1957, the President again authorized overflights over certain important soviet missile and atomic facilities. Eisenhower personally authorized each flight. Lockheed meanwhile, painted the U-2 in a blue-black color that helped it blend against the darkness of space.

In April 1958, The CIA concluded that the U-2 project had a security leak. The source of the leak was never identified, but it was speculated that Lee Harvey Oswald, then a radar operator at a U-2 base in Japan, was the source.

The Soviet launch of Sputnik in October 1957 gave credence to claims of a missile gap between the Soviets and the United States. Some claimed the Soviets might have a three-to-one advantage in ICBMs (InterContinental Ballistic Missiles). The concern over the missile gap caused Eisenhower to reauthorize one Soviet overflight as well as many electronic intelligence gathering (ELINT) flights along the Soviet border. These missions could not confirm or deny the missile gap and Eisenhower authorized one overflight in April 1960. The Soviets, with their advanced radar, were able to quickly track this flight. But despite the greater risk now, the CIA failed to stop the overflights because of overconfidence from the years of successful missions. Eisenhower authorized one more overflight to occur no later than May 1, 1960 because the important Paris Summit would begin May 16.

The 24th deep penetration Soviet overflight occurred on May 1, 1960. It was an ambitious flight plan crossing the Soviet Union. The flight launched from Peshawar, Pakistan, and was to land in Bodo, Norway. Previous flights had always exited in the direction from which they originated. Francis Gary Powers, the most experienced pilot with 27 missions flown, was chosen to fly. The Soviets began tracking the U-2 15 miles outside the border. Over Sverdlovsk, 4 ½ hours into the flight, one of three SA-2 missiles detonated behind the aircraft at 70,000 feet. Another missile hit a Soviet interceptor attempting to reach the U-2. Powers' aircraft was disabled by the missile blast and because of transverse "G" forces he was unable to reach the plane's self-destruct mechanism. He ejected, parachuted to the ground and was quickly captured. The crash did not destroy the U-2 and the Soviets were able to identify much of the equipment. The CIA knew none of this.

The CIA, believing that a U-2 crash would not be survivable, used the pre-existing cover story. On May 3, NASA (the successor to NACA) announced that one of its aircraft, making a high-altitude research flight in Turkey, was missing. It stated that a "weather plane" had strayed off course after its pilot had oxygen difficulties.

By remaining silent, Khrushchev lured the Americans into reinforcing the cover story until he revealed on May 7 that Powers was alive. Eisenhower publicly took full responsibility for the incident on May 11. The Paris Summit collapsed after Khrushchev demanded an apology from the U.S., which Eisenhower refused.

Powers confessed after months of extensive interrogation. In August 1960, he was convicted of espionage and sentenced to three years of prison followed by seven years of hard labor. In February of 1962, Powers was exchanged for Russian spy Rudolf Abel.

Powers returned home but he was criticized for failing to activate the self-destruct system, which would have destroyed the camera, the film, and the classified parts of the airplane. Some officials also criticized him for not using an optional CIA suicide pin hidden inside a hollowed out silver dollar. The CIA, USAF, and Lockheed debriefed Powers extensively. He appeared before the Senate Armed Services Committee. They determined that Powers had followed orders, had not divulged any critical information to the Soviets, and had conducted himself "as a fine young man under dangerous circumstances."

Powers took a job with Lockheed as a test pilot from 1963 to 1970. In 1970, he wrote a book titled "Operation Overflight: a Memoir of the U-2 Incident." The book cast negative publicity on the CIA and Lockheed fired him. He eventually got a job with KNBC, Los Angeles, as a helicopter pilot.

I had gone out to Beale AFB in July 1977 to interview for the U-2 job. While standing around the squadron, we were asked to assemble in the common U-2/SR-71 briefing room to hear a guest speaker. Our mystery guest that day was Francis Gary Powers. He briefed us on his part in the development of the U-2 program and I had a chance to talk to him after the meeting. He felt that it was possible that someone sabotaged his airplane on the ground in Peshawar, Pakistan and that's what brought down his aircraft, not the SA-2 missiles.

About a week later, on August 1, 1977, Powers died in a helicopter crash in the Sepulveda Dam recreation area; he had run out of fuel. According to Powers' son, a mechanic had replaced a faulty fuel gauge without telling Powers, who misread it. At the last moment, he noticed children playing in the area and directed the helicopter away from them. Had he not done this, he might have landed safely.

The U-2 played a prominent role in another Cold War event, The Cuban Missile Crisis. This crisis was the moment the Cold War came closest to turning into nuclear conflict.

In the late summer of 1962, Khrushchev and Castro made a secret agreement to construct several missile sites in Cuba. Scholars have argued about the reason why these missiles were placed there. Some say that Khrushchev didn't really want the missiles in Cuba but was just using them to pressure the U.S. to remove its missiles from Turkey and Italy. Others believe that Castro pressured the Russians to place the missiles there in order to bolster his security against an impending U.S. invasion. Whatever the reason for their placement, they were noticed by the Defense Intelligence Agency, which tasked a U-2 to scan suspected sites. The U-2 brought back evidence of medium and intermediate-range ballistic nuclear missiles only 90 miles from U.S. soil.

    The crisis caused by the evidence of this film brought the world to the brink of nuclear war. President Kennedy ordered a blockade of Cuba to prevent any more arms from entering the country. Several Russian vessels tried to run the blockade, increasing the chance of war between the super powers. Both countries refused to back down, but meanwhile, back-channel negotiations were ongoing between the U.S. and Russia. During these negotiations, a U-2, flown by Major Rudolf Anderson, was shot down over Cuba by a Soviet SA-2 missile. All of President Kennedy's Joint Chiefs called for an invasion of Cuba because of the shoot down. The President did not retaliate and allowed negotiations to continue. The crisis was resolved when the Russians agreed to remove their missiles from Cuba and in return the U.S. secretly agreed to remove its missiles from Turkey and Italy. Major Anderson's body was recovered from Cuba and brought back to his home in South Carolina for burial. He was the first recipient of the Air Force Cross, the second highest military award that the USAF can give. It's awarded for extraordinary heroism to an individual who distinguishes him or herself in combat.

Chapter 3

In July of 1977 my wait was over. I received notice to report to Beale for evaluation. Normally, I was always in good physical condition. I ran, lifted weights, waterskied, and played tennis and racquetball. To prepare for the U-2 medical evaluation, I ramped it up. I increased my running mileage and started running stadium steps as well. I was now training hard six days a week. By the time I left for Beale, I was in the best shape of my life.

The U-2 medical evaluation was essentially the same as NASA's astronaut physical. Everything was evaluated: Cardiovascular health, balance, blood work, vision, and urine were tested. We were even tested to see if we were susceptible to flicker vertigo. This is an imbalance in brain cell activity caused by exposure to low frequency flickering of a bright light. This flickering can cause disorientation, vertigo and nausea. The effects of it are similar to seizures caused by epilepsy. Scientists investigating a series of unexplained helicopter crashes first noticed this phenomenon. Flicker vertigo in a helicopter occurs when the pilot looks up through the blades of the main rotor as it turns in the sun causing the light to strobe. Some people are vulnerable to flicker vertigo and a vulnerable pilot may lose control of his aircraft and/or have a seizure.

To ensure I was mentally healthy, I was thoroughly evaluated by an Air Force psychiatrist. I passed all of his tests.

The most thorough tests were saved for the heart. In addition to all the normal cardiac tests, I was also subjected to a stress EKG. I was hooked up with wires to an EKG machine and placed on a treadmill. The treadmill inclination was set to "0" and I started out with a walking pace. Every three minutes, the treadmill speed increased, as did the incline. I was told to go as long as I could and, since I wanted in this program, I did. After 18 minutes I was running full bore up a steep hill. I had enough and signaled the operator to cut it. He lowered the angle and slowed the speed. When the treadmill stopped I got off but remained attached to the EKG machine. They continued to monitor me for about five more minutes just to see how long it took for my heart to return to normal. The EKG technician said he'd never seen anyone go so long on this test. I was feeling pretty good about the test after that remark. My attitude was about to change.

The cardiologist met with me after the test to go over the results. I expected the doctor would praise my excellent conditioning. Instead he shocked me by telling me that I had the heart of a 45-year old with cardiac ischemia. In layman's terms, it meant that my heart muscle was receiving insufficient blood flow. I was stunned. He showed me the little blips on the paper. Then he calmly told me that I was grounded and I probably would never fly for the Air Force again. I was 29 years old, in the best shape of my life, and my future was crumbling before me. Up to this point, I had passed every physical and mental test they had thrown at me. This made no sense at all. Before leaving the room, the doctor said there might be a way for me to fly again. If I wanted to get back on flying status badly enough, I would have to go to the Brooks Army Medical Center in San Antonio Texas for a "thorough" evaluation. If I passed all of their tests, I would be allowed to fly again. I had no choice. I packed my bags for San Antonio.

The best word I can come up with to describe the process at Brooks would be "exhaustive." This physical lasted two weeks. You can do a lot of testing in two weeks and I had them all. I was at Brooks to have my heart problem evaluated and even though I had passed every other test given at Beale, I still had to undergo every test they had. Every hearing, vision, blood, balance, and mental test was retaken. Plus a few more I hadn't taken previously. One of the additional tests was a radioisotope scan. Radioisotopes were injected into my blood stream. Then I was inserted into what looked like a drawer at the morgue. When the drawer was closed I was in total darkness with my body pressed up against the sides and only a few inches between my face and the lid. They did give me a panic button to use just in case. But now I know what it feels like to be buried alive. I was never really sure if this was really a radioisotope test or a test to measure my panic quotient. I didn't hit the panic button but my thumb remained on it throughout.

One of the lighter moments during those two weeks occurred when I ran across a navigator I had flown with in the C-130. He was at Brooks for an evaluation of an eye problem. We met in the lobby of our temporary quarters and I hardly recognized him. My eyes had been dilated for a macular degeneration test and I couldn't see much of anything. His vision was fine and he called me over when he spotted me. Once I got close enough to him I knew who he was and we caught up on old times. He had a heart monitor attached for a 24-hour EKG. Within a few minutes, the irony of the situation had us both laughing.

No matter what your medical condition is, when you get to Brooks, everything is looked at so they could build their database. So a heart patient with dilated eyes talking to an eye patient with a heart monitor was not unusual.

I retook the stress EKG and once again went 18 minutes. This time the cardiologist who monitored the test told me my heart was perfectly fine. He attributed the previous negative results to an over-developed heart muscle wall. He said this happened frequently in competitive athletes. The wall of the heart thickens and gives off erroneous electrical signals. The next test, an echocardiogram, confirmed this. The echocardiogram showed a view of my beating heart on a video screen. The video screen showed a healthy heart. I was relieved that these tests came out positive, but as my doctor explained to me, they couldn't release me to fly again until I had a cardiac catherization. Even though that first doctor at Beale had been proven wrong, his evaluation was part of my permanent medical record and there was only one way the Air Force would let me fly again. I had to pass the cardiac catherization.

My cardiac catherization was pretty painless but it was stressful. My flying future was on the line and I wanted resounding proof that my heart was disease free. They inserted a catheter into my right inguinal artery. The tube was threaded up into my heart while the doctor and I monitored its progress on a screen. Once in the heart, they pumped dye through the catheter to get a good view of the coronary arteries. The attending doctor declared my heart to be in perfect condition. I was back baby!

Chapter 4

During this whole medical process my family had remained in Selma trying to sell our house. We needed to move regardless of what assignment I received. With San Antonio in my rearview mirror, I made a brief stop at home before flying on to Beale to complete the evaluation process.

The selection process for the U-2 was markedly different than for any other airplane assignment in the Air Force. First of all, it was a "special duty" assignment. For normal assignments, a pilot would fill out an aircraft and base request, commonly referred to as a "dream sheet." This dream sheet listed the airplanes and bases he wanted. The administrators at the Military Personnel Center would choose a base and an airplane, and then send you the results. The pilot had little control over the process. For example, you may have requested an F-4 fighter at MacDill AFB, Florida but you got a B-52 to Minot AFB, North Dakota. To get a special duty assignment, one had to request a slot directly from the unit you wanted to join. If they liked your record, they would invite you out for an evaluation and interview.

The U-2 program called about 10% of all qualified applicants out for an interview. Of those called out, about 10% were accepted into the program after their medical condition and flying skills were evaluated. I was now cleared medically but I still had to demonstrate that I could fly this beast.

The flying evaluation for the U-2 is like none other in the world. Most military aircraft and civilian airlines have simulators for training and candidate evaluation. The U-2 had no simulator. Its flying characteristics are so unique; no simulator could ever duplicate them. To become a pilot in this squadron, you had to demonstrate your ability in the airplane, no simulator warm-ups allowed. For years, there were only single seat U-2s available. The candidate would be thoroughly briefed by an instructor on how to fly the airplane. This interview style resulted in two aircraft accidents. They weren't fatal but the airplanes were damaged. The Air Force decided to find a better way to evaluate U-2 candidates, so they consulted with Lockheed. They took the wrecked airplanes and redesigned them, adding a second cockpit behind the flying pilot. Now an instructor could ride along and prevent the candidate from killing himself and/or wrecking the airplane.

The flying evaluation consisted of one, two, or three flights. If the first flight was really bad and the pilot decided he wanted nothing to do with this airplane, then the evaluation was over and the pilot went home. If the first flight was bad and the pilot wanted to try again, he was given a second ride. If the second ride went well, a third ride tiebreaker was given. However, if the second ride was also bad, the candidate was sent home. If both the first and second rides were good, the pilot was in.

The U-2 evaluation is taken in the "C" model, which has a wingspan of 80 feet. Most airplanes, like the T-38 with a wingspan of 25 feet, have landing gear in a tricycle configuration with one wheel in front and two in back. To save weight, the U-2 was set up like a bicycle with a bigger wheel in front and a smaller one (6 inches) in back. Landing an airplane with this gigantic wingspan is like riding on a tightrope at 90 m.p.h. When on the ground, the huge wings were supported with curved metal mini wing struts called pogos. These struts had a wheel on one end and a metal fitting on the other end. They were attached to the underside of the wings with the fittings at the midpoint of the wing. The pogos kept the wings from scraping the ground during taxi. During takeoff, as soon as the wings developed lift (about 50 knots), the pogos fell out onto the runway. The mobile crew retrieved them and placed them back under the wings after the airplane cleared the runway after landing.

The large wingspan and engine thrust combination made each landing an adventure. The airplane had to be landed in a full stall with the main strut one or two feet above the runway. Landing an airplane this way went against every instinct I possessed. In every other airplane, I would fly down to the runway, gradually decrease power, and then touch down. To make a good U-2 landing, you need to fly down to the runway, throttle back, and then hold the airplane off the ground until it stalled and fell to the runway. My instructor described it as landing a footlocker on the runway, dropped in from two feet. It had to be done this way for two reasons. If you brought the airplane down to the runway without stalling, it would bounce off the runway and leap back into the air. Even with idle thrust, the tremendous lift from the giant wings forced the airplane to keep flying. If on the other hand, you stalled too high (above 2 feet), you risked pushing the main strut up through the fuel tank. So it had to be just right every time. Adding to this complexity were the flight controls. The aircraft had no hydraulics, so operating the flight controls was totally manual. Normal airplanes have hydraulically operated flight controls, usually rated at 3,000 PSI, making them easy to move. Flying the U-2 was like driving a Cadillac with no power steering. Now I would have something in common with those Russian AN-12 pilots - no hydraulics.

To fly the airplane, a yoke was used instead of a stick. The yoke came out of the floor up between the pilot's legs. This yoke took up space in an already cramped cockpit. When I sat in the airplane with the canopy closed, only my hand could fit between the top of my helmet and the canopy. If I raised my elbows up and out, I could touch the sides of the cockpit. The nose of the airplane was especially long. In the landing attitude, you could not see out the front of the airplane. You had to constantly look from side to side to remain aligned with the runway, a skill I had learned on my no flap landings in the T-38.

The airplane was crosswind intolerant. If the crosswind exceeded 10 knots, you had to divert to another airport. In a crosswind, airplanes land using either a 'wing low', or a 'crab' technique. These two techniques are used to keep the airplane centered on the runway when the wind is trying to push you left or right of the centerline. In a normal airplane, using the wing low technique, for a right crosswind, the pilot lines up the airplane fuselage with the centerline using a combination of rightwing down and left rudder. Using the crab technique, the wings are level and the airplane is turned into the wind to prevent drift. With its long wingspan, the U-2 could not use the wing low technique because of the risk of dragging the low wing before touchdown. Landing the U-2 in a crosswind required using the crab technique with one important caveat - you had to be aligned with the runway centerline on touchdown. If you were cocked off, the airplane would instantly align itself on touchdown and possibly snap the steering control on the tail wheel. When this happened you were essentially riding a 50-foot long unicycle that automatically turned into the wind.

Chapter 5

My first ride in the airplane happened on a beautiful September morning in 1977. Beale AFB sits in the Sierra Nevada foothills northeast of Sacramento. The countryside around the airport is stunningly beautiful. The airport has a single 10,000-foot runway. We taxied out to the runway using the taxiway that led us to the center of the runway. This left 5,000 feet available for takeoff. The instructor said he would demo the first takeoff. I was grateful because I had never seen anything remotely like this before. He released the brakes and pushed the throttle to full power. The airplane quickly accelerated, and just as quickly the wings flexed up and the pogos fell out. We accelerated a bit more and the nose started to rise, quickly. A normal airplane's nose will rise to about 10 to 15 degrees above the horizon on takeoff. This one was at 20 degrees, and continuing to 25 degrees, 30 degrees, 35 degrees, 40 degrees, and 45 degrees. This was ridiculous. It finally settled at 45 degrees and stayed there as the runway fell away below us. By the end of the runway (5000 feet), our altimeter was reading 10,000 feet. I had to double-check it but there it was, 10,000 feet and climbing.

We continued our climb to 20,000 feet and leveled off to do some air work. I needed to get a feel for the airplane throughout its speed range. Since there are no hydraulics aiding the flight controls, the airplane felt very different at high speed versus low speed. The airplane responded quickly and easily at high speed. When we slowed down to traffic pattern speed, the effort to move the flight controls dramatically increased. This big Cadillac with wings and no power steering would take some getting used to.

The key to flying any airplane precisely is proper trim control. Trim tabs are small, moveable control surfaces on the wings, rudder and elevator. Controls in the cockpit allow the pilot to move the trim tabs keeping the airplane in balance throughout its speed range. The pilot's goal is to fly the airplane in a certain attitude and speed through proper trim. Ideally, you want to trim for that certain speed, and be able to take your hands off the controls while the airplane remains where you put it.

Cruising along at 250 knots, neutralizing the controls would take some nose down trim. As the airplane slows down to traffic pattern speeds, nose up trim is required. If you leave the airplane trimmed for high speed and then slow down, the nose pitches down trying to maintain the speed it was trimmed for. Proper trimming was especially vital in the U-2. If the airplane was out of trim for a desired speed, you were constantly fighting to keep the airplane where you wanted it.

My instructor took control of the airplane to show me what a typical landing pattern looked like. The first thing required prior to landing was to balance the fuel. The U-2 had three fuel tanks: a center tank and a tank in each wing. Each wing had a five-gallon per minute transfer pump that ported fuel out of the wing into the center tank. The only fuel gauge in the cockpit was a totalizer that showed the total gallons of fuel used. The pilot had no easy way to tell where his fuel was; but you did have to balance it before landing.

In order to determine the balance, the pilot stalled the aircraft. Prior to reaching his destination, the pilot had to slow the airplane down, and then stall it. When the airplane stalled, you noticed which wing fell first. This was the heavier wing since it held more fuel. The next step was to turn on the transfer pump for that wing and balance the fuel. You could tell a seasoned U-2 pilot by looking at his airplane after he landed and cleared the runway. If he had balanced properly, the airplane would sit upright with both wingtips off the ground. An unbalanced airplane would be sitting with one wingtip touching the ground and the other in the air.

Before returning to the Beale airport, my instructor led me through a simulated traffic pattern and landing. At 20,000 feet, the instructor slowed down, the airplane shuttered and stalled with the wings level. Our fuel was balanced. He then accelerated, trimmed the airplane for 90 knots, and rolled into a 45-degree bank to the left. On the simulated downwind, he configured with gear and flaps, holding the 90 knots. From here we started our simulated final turn. We had decided that our imaginary runway was at 18,500 feet. When we reached that altitude, the power came back, the nose came up, and we slowed but held the altitude. Soon the aircraft shook and dropped;

definitely NOT your normal landing. I tried this maneuver a couple of times. Now it was time to return to Beale and try some actual landings.

The normal U-2 traffic pattern was an overhead, racetrack pattern. From three miles out, we'd line up on the runway at 1500 feet above the ground doing 90 knots. Once over the runway, the pilot initiated a 45-degree banked turn and then configured with gear and flaps (still at 90 knots). At the appropriate spot on the downwind leg, the final turn was initiated with the goal being able to arrive over the end of the runway with the main gear six to ten feet in the air still doing 90 knots and aligned with the center of the runway.

Another U-2 pilot in a chase car (known as a Mobile) monitored every U-2 landing. The chase car, an El Camino, sat on the side of the runway entrance waiting for the airplane. As the airplane came over the end of the runway, the chase car accelerated to match the airplane's speed. The chase car pilot called out the main gear altitudes starting at ten feet through touchdown. In addition to the chase car, at Beale, all landings were videotaped and reviewed by the pilots and the operations staff at the end of the day. When you became a pilot in this squadron, you checked your ego at the door. Everybody looked at the tapes and everyone could, and usually did, criticize a poor landing. It was a humbling experience even for the most seasoned pilots. We learned from it and it did improve performance.

The first landing attempt was an instructor demo. Just like we had done out in the area, he brought the airplane down over the runway and then we heard the chase car start his countdown: 10 feet, 8 feet, 4 feet, 2 feet; then a shudder and the airplane settled onto the runway. It was an impressive first landing and two aspects of it struck me. First, the nose was way up in the air. I expected nose high but not this high. I couldn't see anything in front of the airplane. Like the man told me, I had to look from side to side to stay aligned with the runway until touchdown when the nose settled. Second, I had to consciously fight my instincts. Everything I had learned previously about landing airplanes told me to lower the nose and let the airplane land. On this airplane, if I did that before it was ready, it would just bounce and take off again.

Now it was my turn. I took over after takeoff and we flew around the pattern. The airplane seemed like it had a mind of its own, I wanted it to go one way but it had other ideas. "Trim, trim, trim" the instructor said, and I did. Once I had it properly trimmed for 90 knots, things came easier. I brought it around the final turn and lined up on the centerline. The wind was light that day so I didn't have to worry about a crosswind. We came across the threshold and the countdown started: "10 feet, 6 feet, 4 feet" called the chase car. "Don't let it touch" my instructor said, so I held it off. "Two feet" said the chase car. Then it shuttered, sank, and we hit the runway.

The nose fell and I could see again. So we went around and did some more. I ended up with six landings that day. None of them perfect, but all safe and acceptable. After the flight my instructor debriefed me. We reviewed my landing videos along with the Operations Officer, and three other squadron pilots. Everyone offered his comments, both good and bad, but overall it appeared that I did okay.

They set me up with another ride. The second ride went off the following afternoon. The temperature was in the low 90's with about a five-knot crosswind.

Because of its massive wing area, the U-2 is seriously affected by thermals. These are columns of rising air created by uneven heating of the ground from solar radiation. The sun warms the ground, which in turn, warms the air directly above it. Encountering a thermal in a normal airplane causes turbulence, a rough ride. A U-2 encountering a thermal is another story. When the U-2 meets a strong thermal it feels like the airplane is riding up an express elevator. When that rising column of air meets all that wing area, things happen fast. If the pilot doesn't react immediately, the airplane starts climbing, rapidly. This is not a problem when you're in a climb. But in the traffic pattern, when you're 200 feet above the ground trying to hit that six to ten foot window over the end of the runway, it can ruin the whole day.

Immediate corrective action is required. This point was drummed into my head during those flights and briefings. Put the airplane where you want it. Fly the airplane; don't let it fly you. This was the true secret to flying this or any other airplane. When the thermal started pushing you up, you forced the bird back down.

I was thoroughly briefed on this before I flew but I had to see it to believe it. I made the initial takeoff and we proceeded out to the local area to do some basic airwork again. We hit a couple of thermals on climb out but I made a small correction and continued the climb. The basic area work went well so we headed back to the traffic pattern. The instructor demoed the first landing. We did encounter some thermal activity in the final turn and on short final approach. He pointed this out, made the corrections required, and made a nice landing. Now it was my turn. Most of the traffic pattern was normal. We hit a couple of big bumps in the final turn but corrected and continued on. Everything looked wired when I got down on short final approach about 300 feet off the ground. Then we hit a thermal. The airplane started up, quite rapidly. I made a correction but not nearly big or aggressive enough to stop the climb. Within mere seconds we were out of the landing window.

I elected to go around and flew a wide, extended pattern so we could discuss what just happened. But I knew what had happened and I was determined not to repeat it. On the next attempt, we bumped around the final turn and rolled out on final in perfect position. This time the thermal hit about 100 feet higher than the last time but I was ready. I aggressively pushed the airplane back down to the glide path adjusting the throttle to keep the airspeed right at 90 knots. This time we were able to land. Because of the crosswind I did land in a slight crab. I thought my instructor was going to come through the Plexiglas separating the front and rear cockpits and gnaw my head off. Jesus H. Christ, I thought. I beat the thermal, made the landing, and he's still reaming me a new asshole. We talked about that for a while. I had learned my lesson. EVERY landing had to be done just right every time. Speed had to be exact, altitude over the end of the runway precise, and crab, none allowed. We did six more and I had found my groove, all good landings, and no crab. When that flight was over I was sure of two things. I had made the program, and I was completely wrung out, exhausted, and sweat-soaked.

My instructor debriefed me, congratulated me and we made the rounds in the squadron. Every pilot in the building congratulated me and welcomed me to the most exclusive flying club on earth.

I called my wife with the good news and she gave me her good news. We had a buyer for our house. What a day!

Chapter 6

I returned to Selma to start the big move. Seven days later we were ready to hit the road. We were a two-car family and that complicated the trip. Doreen and the kids took the station wagon while I drove the TR-6. We each had a CB radio and had our own mini caravan across the country. It's hard to imagine making a trip like that today without cell phones but the CB worked well for us. We took frequent breaks and made it into a short vacation.

Base housing at Beale was considerably nicer and newer than either Pope or Craig. Since off-base housing was quite a distance from the base, we opted to move into Officers housing at Beale. Our house sat on a ridge looking out over beautiful, rolling hills.

Once we settled into our house, I began the mind-numbing process of checking into a new base. This consisted of carrying around a large stack of official documents from building to building getting every administrator's seal of approval.

We were also meeting our neighbors. We had a good group on our street. My next-door neighbor was an SR-71 pilot, Major Tom Peck. Tom had been on base for a year but hadn't flown yet. Our wing, the 9th Strategic Reconnaissance Wing, included the U-2 and the SR-71. Both squadrons were housed in a large "H" shaped building. The U-2 operation on one side, the SR-71 group on the other, with a common operations briefing room in the middle.

The SR-71, nicknamed the "Blackbird," was the fastest airplane on earth. Huge, black, and twin-engine, it could cruise at three times the speed of sound. It looked like something from the set of Star Wars. Naturally, in such elite groups as ours, there was intense rivalry. The U-2 was a single engine, single pilot aircraft. Our unofficial motto was "Alone, Unarmed, and Unafraid." Both squadrons' pilots wore orange flight suits. No other USAF pilots did. We thought we were the "Cat's Ass."

The SR-71 was a two-man operation, a pilot up front and a systems operator in the back. It was our one pilot, one engine operation versus their two-man, two engine operation. Obviously we were superior to them! The SR-71 got all the publicity: newspapers, national magazines, radio and TV interviews. We referred to their squadron as the 1st SPS or Strategic Publicity Squadron. They were always on national news setting a new Los Angeles to Washington speed record. Kelly Johnson at Lockheed, the designer of the U-2, also designed the SR-71. The airplane was built to do post-nuclear war strike damage assessment. Since it never got to do that, they had to think of other things for it to do. Setting speed records was one of them.

The U-2 was the airplane of choice for aerial reconnaissance. It was a stable platform and provided outstanding results. The SR-71 was very fast but the quality of its product didn't measure up to the U-2's results. The SR-71 was also a maintenance nightmare. During supersonic flight, the titanium-skinned airplane stretched out more than 18 inches. When the airplane taxied out before flight it leaked fuel like a sieve. Once the airplane got airborne and heated up, it sealed up and the leaks stopped. Every time it flew, it required a complete maintenance phase inspection. In laymen's terms, they practically took the airplane apart and put it back together after each flight. After learning these facts about the airplane, it became clear to me why Peck still hadn't flown after being here a year.

Chapter 7

One of the perks of joining this select group was the additional flying available, not in the U-2 but in the T-38. Both U-2 and SR-71 pilots had twelve T-38s to use to maintain instrument currency, go cross-country, or fly formation. Since I was a certified T-38 instructor at Craig, I was now a T-38 instructor at Beale.

All USAF pilots are required to take an annual instrument check either in the airplane or the simulator. The U-2 had no simulator. Since it was cheaper and easier to schedule, the squadron was given special permission to give U-2 pilots their annual instrument check in the T-38. Flying the T-38 at Beale was an exciting job. We acted as chase ship for the SR-71. Quite frequently the Blackbird would return from its mission with something wrong. A chase ship would be sent up to meet the airplane and fly formation with it. This allowed the pilot of the T-38 to look for leaks, hanging panels, popped fasteners, or anything else that might have broken on the airplane. It was quite the rush to fly formation with an airplane three times your size. The SR-71 engines had big spikes that would move in and out during flight regulating the air intake. Whenever I flew alongside this behemoth I felt like one of those remoras that feed off of a great white shark - small, insignificant, but staying close.

Now that I was officially in the squadron, I began the training to become a fully qualified U-2 pilot. The latest, operational version of the U-2 I would eventually fly was the "R" model. The "R" is a huge airplane. It has a wingspan of 103 feet, a length of 63 feet, all powered by 18,500 pounds of thrust from its Pratt and Whitney J-75 engine. The empty weight of the airplane is still classified but on traffic pattern-only training missions, the airplane had more thrust than weight. In 1977 all the Rs were single seat airplanes so I would initially train on the two-seat "C" model. The C-model was the earlier, smaller version of the R with only an 80-foot wingspan.

The training syllabus included five flights. The first two in the two-seat model, followed by a solo ride in the single seat U-2C. The training ended with two more solo rides in the C.

I was excited about the first ride. It would be my first high flight and was something I had wanted for a long time. My two evaluation flights had been low altitude, only up to 20,000 feet. This flight was meant to introduce me to the real purpose of the airplane, high altitude flying. For all non-high flights, the pilot wears a normal flight suit and helmet.

High altitude flying required a pressure suit. Pressure suits were needed to keep the pilot at a safe cabin altitude. The U-2 flew above 70,000 feet so the pilot needed to be protected in case of cabin pressure loss. The U-2 cabin was normally maintained at 28,000 feet but if the engine failed or the canopy cracked, the cabin would rapidly rise to the actual altitude of the airplane. Without the protection of the pressure suit, the pilot would quickly die.

One of the most important support organizations in the wing was the Physiological Support Division (PSD). The PSD maintained all the pressure suits and dressed us prior to a high flight. Putting on a pressure suit isn't as easy as slipping on a flight suit.

The average U-2 high flight lasted about 10 hours and everyone started at the PSD building. The pilot would show up about two hours prior to flight. Pilots were fed a high protein, low fat meal. Then the dressing process began.

The technicians pre-tested the pressure suit for leaks, tears or malfunctions before they helped the pilot climb into it. All U-2 and SR-71 pilots had two custom fitted suits. In 1977 these pressure suits were valued at $100,000 each.

The dressing process began with the pilot donning a long-john pant and shirt combination. To enable the pilot to urinate in flight, he wore a condom-like device with a long plastic tube attached to the end. The plastic tube would extend from the pressure suit and eventually was connected to the airplane. The pilot connected the condom and tube to the pants with Velcro. Once this was complete, the pilot presented himself to the PSD technicians.

The technicians did the real work in dressing the pilot. The pilot merely followed their instructions to sit, stand, or turn while the technicians maneuvered the suit and secured him inside. Once the pressure suit was on, the helmet was attached.

Now that the pilot was properly dressed in the pressure suit he was placed in a recliner and hooked up to air conditioning and 100% oxygen. This was the start of his one-hour of pre-breathing.

One hour of pre-breathing was required to rid the body of any excess nitrogen, which could cause the "bends." The bends is also known as decompression sickness and describes a condition occurring when dissolved gases come out of the blood and form bubbles inside the body. These bubbles can migrate to any part of the body causing a variety of results from pain and rashes to paralysis and even death. Pre-breathing 100% oxygen would eliminate virtually all of the gases from the pilot's body. Since the U-2 pilot flew at a cabin altitude of 28,000 feet, pre-breathing was imperative to prevent the bends. Modern airliners are pressurized at a cabin altitude of between six and eight thousand feet so "bends" is not an issue for the travelling public.

The PSD building had several recliners to choose from. I remember sitting in one of the recliners for my pre-breathe prior to my first high flight. I was both anxious and excited. Anxious because I was about to experience something that few men before me ever had and I wanted a successful mission with no problems. Excited because of the prospect of seeing the world from a new vantage point.

With pre-breathing complete, the pilot was escorted to a waiting PSD van for transport to the aircraft. Portable oxygen and air conditioning units were attached to the suit for the ride to the airplane.

Once the pilot was seated in the cockpit, the technicians connected him to the aircraft's oxygen and air conditioning systems. They also connected the urine drain line from the suit. This line would be secured into a well that sat underneath the control column and had a two-quart capacity. The technicians completed the process by attaching the seat belt and shoulder harness.

The U-2C required a different pressure suit than the R model. The C-suit was a "squeeze" suit. This meant that if the airplane lost cabin pressure, the suit would squeeze or constrict the pilot. The R-suit, used only in the U-2R, would inflate with a cabin pressure loss. The R-suit is the same suit worn by the space shuttle astronauts. Both suits had the same purpose of keeping the pilot at a 28,000 feet cabin pressure.

Personally, I disliked the C-suit. It was skin-tight, restrictive and uncomfortable. The R-suit was a vast improvement over the older C-suit. The R-suit was loose fitting and inflatable. In flight, with a push of a button, you could inflate the suit and move around inside it. Since I would be flying the U-2C in my upcoming high flights it meant I had to wear the uncomfortable C-suit.

Chapter 8

The itinerary for the first mission would take us north out of Beale up to the Crater Lake area of Oregon, then southeast to Elko, Nevada, and southwest back to Beale. This mission's emphasis was in navigation. The weather was beautiful in all directions and we blasted off into the cloudless California sky. The climb rate of the airplane was amazing. The instructor pointed out that we didn't have a full fuel load and we had no payload (normally cameras) on board. These two factors had a significant effect on the aircraft's climb rate. The altimeter spun around quickly as the ground fell away below us; 40,000 feet, 50,000, 60,000, then 65,000 feet. As we climbed, the view from my seat changed dramatically. From this altitude, I could clearly see the curvature of the earth. The sky was no longer its normal blue, but was now a rich, dark purple color. I could see 500 miles in every direction and I felt like I was on top of the world. As I gazed out at the distant horizon, the beauty of the panorama overwhelmed me. I felt truly humbled and grateful to be able to see this magnificence. I had never experienced such a scene in my entire life and I still recall it exactly as it happened, 38 years ago.

Navigating in the U-2 was easier than I thought it would be. Normal airplanes, when navigating from one point to another, had to correct for wind. Without constant correction, the wind would push the airplane off course. This was not a concern in the U-2 because there is no wind above 50,000 feet. Your heading to the target is automatically your course. One of the other nice navigation aids was the reverse periscope. It worked just like a periscope on a submarine but instead of being able to see up, you could see what was directly below you. One of the systems the airplane didn't have, and I thought I would miss, was the weather radar. It turned out that I didn't need it, at least at high altitude. If there was a thunderstorm along the route, I could usually top it. This would later prove to be a problem at night however.

The inflight refreshments in the U-2 were very limited. It was very important to stay hydrated. Pint-sized bottles of water or Gatorade were provided. Attached to the top of these bottles was a long, flexible plastic tube, which fit into an opening in the front of the helmet. I followed my instructor's advice and drank plenty of liquid during the flight. This is where I encountered my first problem in the airplane. I drank, and I drank, and I drank some more; but I couldn't urinate in the airplane. I absolutely could not make myself do it. As hard as I tried and as much as I wanted to, it would not flow. I think I couldn't get over the idea of peeing in my pants. Rationally, I know that the urine would flow into the tube and down into the well, but my body wouldn't believe it.

We completed our navigation and now it was time to start down. The U-2 doesn't like to go down. It was designed to go up, to climb. The

combination of thrust and wing area made descent difficult. The descent checklist read as follows:
1. Power: Idle
2. Landing Gear: Down
3. Flaps: Extend
4. Speed Brakes and Spoilers: Extend

Even with all this stuff hanging off the airplane, it still took 45 minutes to an hour to get back to Mother Earth. Meanwhile, I really had to pee, but still couldn't do it in the airplane. I had to wait until I got back to the PSD building and undressed. Ahhhh, relief!

The second training flight followed a pattern similar to the first, only this time; we headed down the coast of California, east to Death Valley, then back to Beale. I knew I had to beat this urination problem. Once again I drank plenty of fluids hoping to force the issue, but it was still a no-go. I returned to the Beale traffic pattern with a full bladder.

The crosswind that day was just under the limit at 9 or 10 knots and we had to practice landings. The first landing was successful but we landed in a very slight crab. The second time we landed in a crab again but more pronounced this time. When the airplane touched down, it immediately realigned itself with the runway. That's when the fun started.

As advertised, with that sudden correction, the tailwheel steering had snapped. We knew this because the airplane started turning into the crosswind like a weathervane and was not responding to tailwheel steering inputs. The instructor took control of the airplane as we continued to drift right. He shut down the engine as we ran off the runway into the grass. We stopped about 20 feet off the runway and let tower know what was happening. We told them we didn't need an emergency response. Our mobile crew had seen what had happened and they arranged for a tug to bring the aircraft back to the maintenance hangar. I experienced first hand what a tailwheel failure felt like. The airplane turned into the wind and we were powerless to do anything about it.

The third mission was solo day. It was strictly a traffic pattern ride so no pressure suit was required. The weather was clear but it was windy. On my first landing attempt, I stalled it a bit too low and the airplane hit the runway and became airborne again. I went around and tried it again. This time I wasn't lined up properly. The crosswind was light but I was still turned into the wind as I held the airplane off the ground. I didn't like the look of it so I went around again. Now I was talking to myself. I gave myself a good pep talk and went at it again. This time it all came together for a successful landing. I completed three more that day before it was time to quit. The Wing and Squadron Commanders, as well as the base photographer that documented the deed, met me as I climbed down from the cockpit. I had become the 258th person to solo the U-2. It was a great milestone for me and I was awfully glad it was behind me.

That night there was a ceremony in my honor at the Officers Club in which I was officially inducted into the U-2 pilot fraternity. To make it legal, I had one more chore to perform. Every new U-2 pilot had to do it and now it was my turn.

A yard of beer was filled to the top (and I mean all the way to the top). A small, black U-2 pin was dropped to the bottom of the yard glass. My task was to lift the yard without spilling a drop of beer and drink it all down without lowering the yard. I had to keep the yard up until it was empty and the pin slid into my mouth. This was way harder than flying the airplane, but with all the squadron pilots shouting their encouragement, I managed to do it. Luckily, I had the next day off to recover.

The next two C missions were solo high flights similar to the ones I had previously flown with an instructor. These two missions had a different feel. There was definitely something different about being alone up there. I can only describe it as blissful isolation. It was just me and the airplane flying along as one, 14 miles above the earth. On a more mundane note, I still couldn't pee.

On the last C flight I was determined to make it work. I forced the issue. I drank at least a quart of water before I suited up. Additionally, I drank three bottles of Gatorade and two bottles of water in flight. Just when I thought my bladder would burst, I was able to go. What blessed relief! Once I had gone while in the pressure suit the first time, all bets were off. I was so comfortable going in the suit that I had no difficulty going anytime, including when the technicians were strapping me in before departure. They would give me this look like, "couldn't you wait until we were gone before you let loose?" I just smiled and let it flow.

It was during these last two "C" flights that I was introduced to the U-2 version of the boxed lunch. In the cockpit, beneath my left elbow, was a small, round hole in the panel. This was the oven. The food came in tubes resembling toothpaste tubes. I popped a tube into the oven, turned it on, and waited. After a few minutes I took the tube out of the oven and screwed a plastic bayonet on the end of the tube. I inserted the bayonet end into the hole in my helmet and started squeezing the food through the tube into my mouth. Some of the meals available were spaghetti and meatballs, pot roast, macaroni and cheese and even butterscotch pudding for dessert. I never came back from a mission hungry. In spite of eating the tube food and drinking five or six bottles of water or Gatorade, I would lose an average of five pounds on a typical ten-hour mission.

Chapter 9

After completing the five "C" missions, I graduated to the "R." The U-2R was a very different flying machine from the "C." The "R" was heavier, had a longer fuselage and 23 more feet of wing. This was the airplane in operational use around the world. I was scheduled for five training flights out of Beale before I would be eligible for an overseas TDY. Since there were no "R" trainers, a thorough briefing from an instructor before the mission would have to suffice. The cockpits of the "C" and "R" were similar but not identical. We didn't have a simulator or mock up for the "R" so I spent several hours sitting in the actual airplane familiarizing myself with the switch locations. The "R" is an ominous looking beast. The airplane is painted with a special radar-reflective black paint. The only thing clearly visible on the airplane is the five-digit registration number painted in red on the tail.

My first flight in the "R" was a traffic pattern only ride. As soon as I began to taxi I could feel the "R" was different. It felt more sluggish and harder to maneuver on the ramp. Every turn required a bigger lead point. The "C" was difficult enough to taxi; the "R" was more so. With only a steerable tailwheel the longer wings and fuselage demanded your complete attention while on the ground. I managed to get myself out to the runway without running off the taxiway. I was cleared for takeoff and lined the airplane up with the centerline of the runway. I ran the engine up, checked the gauges and released the brakes. The airplane shot forward like it was launched from a catapult. The pogos dropped off immediately and I was airborne.

Since I was staying in the traffic pattern, I leveled at 1500 feet and set up for the first landing. I soon discovered that the "R" was more sluggish in the air as well as on the ground. It took more effort to muscle it around the pattern. This airplane was made to fly above 70,000 feet. To its designers, flying it around the traffic pattern was an afterthought. The airplane did trim up nicely and soon I felt more comfortable flying it. The first landing proved to be a non-event. The heavier, wider airplane worked to my advantage. The "C" model was very unstable in the longitudinal axis (front to back), and would easily porpoise on landing. The "R" was a rock and didn't jump around like the "C."

I was much happier with my "R" landings. All the caveats of the "C" landing still applied but the heavier airplane produced consistently better landings. I cleared the runway after my last landing and stopped on the taxiway. The airplane settled on the left wingtip. Each wingtip has a replaceable titanium skid for this reason. As my proficiency increased, I would eventually be able to clear the runway and wait for my mobile to install the pogos without either wingtip touching the ground.

My next mission would be a get acquainted high flight. The airplane flew differently at high altitude and I had to become as comfortable flying high as I was at traffic pattern altitude.

The airplane was made to fly high. A quick way to verify this fact is to look at the operation of the autopilot. The autopilot worked well for both navigation and basic aircraft control such as turns, climbs, and descents. But it was only effective above 50,000 feet. From ground level up to 50,000 feet, it was worthless. If you engaged the autopilot below 50,000 feet, it simply didn't follow the pilot's inputs.

The most critical factor on a U-2 high flight was speed control. If not strictly controlled it could kill you. The mission profile is a constant climb that shallows out the higher you go. After nine or ten hours, you're at 75,000 feet and it's time to go home.

Above 50,000 feet, the autopilot was engaged and set for the ideal climb speed. This speed was somewhere between 100 and 110 knots indicated airspeed (IAS). The true airspeed at high altitude was 406 knots. At sea level with no wind, the indicated and true airspeeds are virtually identical. True airspeed corrected for instrument and position error, then adjusted for dynamic pressure differences, yields the indicated airspeed. The airspeed in the climb was critical for two reasons. If the speed was too slow, just five knots below target speed, the airplane would stall. The entire tail assembly of the airplane (rudder and elevator) was held in place by three bolts. A high altitude stall would violently drop the airplane and the tail would separate. The low altitude stalls we did to balance the fuel load prior to landing were not risky, the high altitude ones were. If the aircraft exceeded the climb speed by only five knots, it would experience Mach buffet, which would violently shake the airplane and lead to the same result as a stall, loss of the tail.

The autopilot did a pretty good job of speed control but it had to be closely monitored because your life depended on it.

During the extended climb, engine exhaust gas temperature (EGT) had to be kept as high as possible without over temping the engine. This was done to get maximum performance from the airplane. If engine EGT was exceeded, a small red light on the gauge would illuminate. The U-2 had no auto throttle. It was manual control only. If the EGT was set to the limit, it would stay there for a few minutes, then creep higher, eventually tripping the warning light on. For the entire mission prior to descent the pilot had to continuously crack the throttle back to remain within EGT limits. Combine the critical speed control with the equally critical EGT control and you can see how a U-2 pilot could become "task saturated" very easily.

The first U-2R high flight ended without drama, but I did discover an interesting detail about the urine collection system. Since I was now very comfortable urinating through my suit, I drank a lot in flight. This particular mission was about five hours long and I had five bottles of Gatorade. I also had some water before I suited up. About three hours into the mission, while recycling this fluid from myself to the airplane, I noticed a yellow fluid shooting out of a thin tube on the back of the control column. I followed this tube down and it led into the urine collection box. What no one had bothered to tell me was that when the box filled up, the excess urine shot out through the overflow tube up onto the canopy just above my head. Since the canopy was cold from being at altitude, the pee froze. Now I had a sheet of yellow ice hanging over my head. On descent, as the outside air temperature warmed, the pee liquefied and started raining down on me. I was going to say this really pissed me off, but…

    The next high flight added a new wrinkle to my training. This flight would be for photo reconnaissance. The nose of the U-2R is very long and built to hold a variety of cameras. The one loaded on my airplane that day was the most advanced model available. It was huge. The tech guys said it was the size of a Volkswagen. A special nose cone was fitted on the plane to accommodate this monster. The lower part of the nose cone had clear Plexiglas panels along the axis of the lens. When the camera was on, the entire nose cone rotated from left to right and back again. While rotating continuously, the camera took pictures from horizon to horizon all along the flight path.

    My route that day took me west to Delta, Utah, just southwest of Provo. From there I turned south to Tucson. This track would take me about 50 miles east of Phoenix. I turned the camera on as I passed abeam Phoenix and I watched in amazement as the entire nose of the airplane rotated left, right and back again. When I hit the southern limits of the city I turned off the camera and wondered what kind of pictures I had taken.

Later that week I met with the Photo Intel people so I could view my work. The most striking pictures I remember were taken of a parking lot at the University of Phoenix at Tempe. From 50 miles east and above 70,000 feet, the license plates on the cars in the lot were easily readable.

During my non-flying days, my wife and I spent the time acclimating to northern California. The location was great for more than just the beautiful weather. We were within easy driving distance to the Lake Tahoe/Reno area to the east, and San Francisco to the southwest. We also got to spend some time getting to know the neighbors.

One neighbor, who lived behind us, had been overseas when we arrived and he had just returned from a remote temporary duty at Osan Air Base, Korea. "Muff" Johansen was a short but powerful hulk of a man. He had been in the squadron about two years before I arrived. He was a wealth of information on both the airplane and life in Korea.

I made it a point to get to know every squadron pilot. Not only would I eventually work with them, I believed they each could add to my knowledge of the U-2 operation. They all had unique experiences in the airplane and I wanted to know about them. If, for example, I had talked to enough pilots I may have found out about the "pee" shower before experiencing it. The seasoned veterans in the squadron, however, believed that all new guys should experience these non-critical "eye openers" for themselves.

Muff had several nuggets of information to share. The U-2, in addition to its Photo Recon and Electronic INTelligence (ELINT) missions, was often tasked to fly special missions for the Department of Agriculture. Muff had flown one of these missions. He surveyed a large swath of western Kansas that was to be evaluated for a proposed water distribution system for large farm operations. Muff had flown out to Kansas, done the survey, and was on his way back to Beale when things went awry. He was about 100 miles out at 72,000 feet when he pulled the power back to descend and the engine quit. Muff was not in a hurry; he knew the glide ratio of the airplane so he wasn't concerned about making it back to Beale.

The glide ratio compares how many feet forward the aircraft will fly for every foot it descends while gliding. For example, an aircraft with a glide ratio of 2:1 will fly two feet forward for every foot it descends; alternatively, a rock has a glide ratio of 0:1. The U2 has a glide ratio of 23:1, which gives it a range of a little over 300 miles. Muff continued toward the airport, ran through his checklists and considered his options. Since the airplane had no hydraulic flight controls it flew exactly the same with the engine running or shut down, so he had that going for him. The weather was good and he could comfortably reach Beale, so there was no reason for him to try to go anywhere else. As he descended, he kept trying to restart the engine. He tried five starts, all failed. As he came through 10,000 feet he tried one more, and this time it worked. He landed uneventfully and handed the airplane over to maintenance.

The next story he told me didn't come out as neatly as the first one. This one occurred while he was overseas at Osan Air Base, Korea. Muff's mission was to monitor a North Korean munitions test. This was a high priority mission that our Intel people had to have. Muff had an early morning departure and he was expected to be airborne for about eight hours. The previous night he had a generous helping of the Korean specialty, Kimchi, which is made by sealing cabbage, daikon radishes, and several potent spices in clay vessels. These jars are then buried in the ground for months to cure. Kimchi can be very spicy.

Muff felt fine the next morning as he prepared for his flight. He ate his normal pre-flight breakfast and did his one-hour of pre-breathing. He continued to feel good until about two hours into the mission. The spicy Korean cabbage was definitely causing some distress south of the border - Muff's, not the Korean's.

He knew he was in trouble but the mission was too important to abort. He felt the irresistible urge and fought it as long as he could. He finally surrendered and dumped in his suit. This was not good. At that point he still had over five hours to go, so he sat in it and flew the mission as planned. By the time he returned, he was in agony. He spent the next four days at the base hospital being treated for a severe case of adult diaper rash. And they had to throw away his pressure suit.

Another fellow U-2 pilot was Rich Boyle. Rich was the first person I met when I came to Beale to start my medical evaluation. Rich had been in the squadron about 15 months. He acted as my squadron liaison and introduced me to the squadron staff. When I arrived at Beale in July 1977, Rich had just returned from a two month TDY in Cyprus. The primary Cyprus mission was monitoring the Middle East peace. Egypt, Israel, Lebanon and Syria had all agreed to allow U-2 overflights. A thorough photo recon of the entire area ensured that no one was cheating on the peace accords. Since none of the signees knew when a mission would be launched it kept all the players honest.

While in Cyprus, Rich was scheduled for a high priority mission. This was a photo recon mission scheduled to fly up through Turkey, then northeast along the Bulgarian and Romanian border. He wasn't told what he was looking for, only that his route of flight was strictly controlled with no deviations permitted. This type of high security mission through multiple borders and international waterways required diplomatic clearances from all countries involved, and was not easily obtainable. The State Department was able to get these clearances but it took over six months to do so. Once the clearances were obtained, the flight was arranged and Rich would fly it. The eight-hour flight was scheduled to depart in the early morning. The photo target of this flight was in Eastern Romania.

The squadron navigators would prepare 8 ½" x 11" green waypoint boards for the pilots. These boards listed the overfly waypoints from top to bottom. Special instructions for each waypoint were marked along the right-hand column of the card. When the pilot reached the last waypoint on a card, he selected the next card and worked his way down it. The highest number of cards I've seen was eight.

One of the important remarks along the side of the card was "camera on." Rich reached the point in the mission and saw the "camera on" prompt. He reached over and engaged the switch. The switch had three positions: OFF, NEUTRAL, and ON. When the camera switch was ON, a small green light next to it illuminated. Rich continued following the waypoint boards until he saw the "camera off" prompt. He reached for the switch and was shocked at the absence of the green light. Unfortunately for Rich, he had placed the switch in the NEUTRAL position. The camera was never turned on.

That's when the awful truth washed over him. All this mission planning, international clearances, and State Department negotiations were wasted. All the hard work by the support staff, the navigators, the maintenance people who prepared the airplane, and the back-up pilot had all been for naught. There was no do-over. He couldn't turn around and try it again. This was a one-time clearance and he had FUBARed it

(Fucked Up Beyond All Recognition). He had the whole way back to Cyprus to think about it. He couldn't feel any worse than he did. It took Rich a long time to forgive himself for that one.

My neighbor across the street was also in my squadron. Major Dave "Doc" Hall was the official old guy in the squadron. He actually had grey hair. He had been around a while and had seen some interesting things. Doc had two experiences he was willing to share with me. The first one concerned a flight he had taken two years earlier.

This flight departed from Diego Garcia. This footprint-shaped atoll is located south of the equator in the central Indian Ocean. It is part of the British Indian Ocean Territory. The U.S. Navy operates the Naval Support Facility that includes an air base. Diego Garcia is about as remote a location as one can imagine. It sits in the middle of the ocean with nothing else around it for hundreds of miles. Doc had flown down there earlier in the week from Cyprus. He was positioned there to fly a photo recon mission over Somalia, East Africa. Diego Garcia was the closest launch point for a Somalia mission. Flight planning was crucial because of the fuel supply. One of the factors Doc had to consider on this flight was his navigation planning. His Omega navigation system, the primary system he would use on this flight, had been written up on a previous flight as being inoperative. Maintenance had fixed it and signed off on it.

The long flight to and from Somalia would take about 9 hours and 30 minutes. This left only about one hour for photo recon once he reached the target. The flight over to Somalia took 4 hours and 45 minutes. Doc spent about 45 minutes photographing the target. He finished his photo run and turned back out to sea; Diego Garcia was 4 hours and 45 minutes away. This was the beginning of a stressful series of events that would make for a long night.

A very thick cloud layer had rolled into Diego Garcia. Everything within 200 miles of the airfield was covered from 500 feet above the ground up to around 5,000 feet. As he headed east from the coast of Africa, his Omega failed. He would normally now be relying on his backup system, the Tactical Air Navigation (TACAN). The U-2 used TACAN in the weather. Military aircraft used TACAN and it was more accurate than VOR/DME systems used by civilian aircraft. TACAN provided bearing and range information to the aircraft. Diego Garcia had a TACAN station but it was off the air for maintenance repair. So his two primary navigation aids were inoperative.

Doc would be arriving at night and would have to rely on the station's radar to guide him through the clouds and down to the runway. Prior to his arrival, Diego Garcia's radar failed. Doc now had nothing to guide him down but he also had no place else to go. When Doc had first arrived in Diego Garcia, he had been briefed about the treacherous Indian Ocean surrounding the base.

Foremost among his concerns were the sharks and he didn't want to ditch into shark-infested waters.

Doc had received the news about the radar outage through his secure High Frequency radio when he was still 150 miles out. Navigating above 50,000 feet was pretty straightforward. Since there was no wind up there Doc simply held the heading he thought would lead him to the airport. Below 50,000 feet, he had to factor the wind into his navigation. This would be a combination of guesswork and good luck. He knew he had to come up with a plan to get down and see the airport. He planned on an early descent. He wanted the airport ahead of him when he broke out of the cloud deck. This strategy would cost him valuable fuel but if he broke out with the airport behind him, he may never find it, fuel or no fuel. He planned to break out of the clouds at 500 feet and hoped that the airport would be just a few miles ahead of him.

Once he started down, he noted his low fuel supply; he didn't have a lot to play with. He was able to establish radio contact with the tower as he entered the cloud layer at 5,000 feet. He had every light in the airplane on hoping that if he couldn't see the runway, the tower would see him and direct him toward the airport. Down through the clouds he came, from 5,000 feet all the way down to 500 feet, waiting to break out and still nothing. He checked his vanishing fuel supply and went down another 100 feet. He finally broke out of the bottom of the cloud deck and saw... nothing. Before him was a vast black hole. He tried to keep his voice under control. It was one thing to die a horrible death in shark-infested waters, but Doc was not going to sound like a wimp as he did so. He kept talking to tower as he searched the horizon for a light but there was nothing ahead of him.

    Just as he decided to turn back in the other direction, the tower called saying they might have spotted him. They asked him to start a left turn to verify that it was him that they saw. He started turning and tower confirmed his sighting. He stayed in the turn until he could see the airport. The final piece of bad news at the end of this grueling 12-hour day was the wind report. Tower was reporting a 15-knot direct crosswind; the limit for the U-2 was 10 knots. But his choices were limited. He had to put the airplane down here or dump it in the drink with the sharks. He opted for the runway. He headed directly to it. He had no fuel to waste in setting up a long, straight-in approach. The landing was as good as it gets but not good enough. In order to keep from drifting away from the runway and into the ocean, he had to hold the crab on landing. The airplane settled on the runway and immediately aligned itself, snapping the tailwheel steering. Since the same thing had happened to me on a training ride, I knew exactly what was coming. His airplane turned into the wind and ran off the side of the runway. Doc was so thankful and relieved to be on the ground and not in the ocean he neglected to shut off the engine. He stopped the airplane and only then did he think about the running engine.

As he reached for the shutoff switch, the engine shut itself down. He had run out of fuel.

Doc's other experience was a much more uplifting, feel-good story. While at Beale, Doc had been assigned a search and rescue mission over the Pacific Ocean. In October of 1976, Doc joined in the search for a seaman who had been adrift for three weeks. The seaman was the sole survivor of a shipwreck and he was thought to be adrift in an orange raft.

Doc's mission was to scour the Pacific by taking recon photos of the seaman's suspected track. It was hoped that an analysis of Doc's film would show the raft's position. Doc spent several hours crisscrossing the suspect area. He returned to the base and was met by the photo interpreters who retrieved the film from his airplane. From 70,000 feet over an ocean that appeared nearly pitch black the raft was spotted. It was a mere bright speck in a dark frame. Due to Doc's efforts, the lost sailor was brought safely home.

Chapter 10

Once I finished my training in the U-2R, I continued to build time by flying missions out of Beale. I needed to build this time before I could go TDY to one of the remote locations.

On my last Beale flight prior to my first TDY I had a revealing experience at the Physiological Support Division (PSD) building. I returned from a six-hour mapping mission and was in the PSD building getting out of my suit. One of the two technicians helping me undress was new to the unit. Sgt. Laura Mayall was a lovely, shy young lady about 22 years old. The suit had been unzipped from the back and I was standing straight up as Laura and her older fellow technician tried to pull the suit off. Normally, after the techs unzip the suit and get the top half off, they leave the room to give the pilot privacy as he undoes the bottom and removes the urine collection tube.

On this day, however, the suit was stuck on my shoulders. Laura pulled on the sleeves but it wouldn't come off. Both techs grabbed the shoulders of the suit and gave one big yank. The suit came off so suddenly that Laura fell on her knees in front me with her head about a foot in front of my crotch. The suit had come all the way off and so had my urine collection tube. Laura looked shocked as she stared at my manhood so close to her face. She made a little screaming noise and quickly left the room. It all happened so fast that I didn't even realize that I was exposed until she had left the room and I looked down to see what all the fuss was about. She quickly recovered and from then on we had something to laugh about.

The typical U-2 pilot spent about half his time overseas. New pilots were always sent to Osan Air Base, Korea, as their first TDY. By January of 1978 I had accumulated enough hours to go to Korea.

January in Korea was brutal. The weather was always cold and bleak. I thought the country and its people were fascinating but these positives didn't overcome the lousy weather. I soon settled into my BOQ and learned my way around the base and the local area surrounding it. Our Korea detachment was small, consisting of an Operations Officer (the Boss), three pilots, and one airplane. Unlike other TDY locations, we wore our uniforms on base. Officially, we weren't there but everyone on base knew about the U-2. The airplane flew two or three times a week. That meant I would fly once a week at a maximum, and act as mobile, or launch supervisor, once a week.

Osan is located about 25 miles south of Seoul, the largest city and capital of South Korea. The base itself is just south of the small town of Osan. If you were in the market for custom clothing, Seoul, and even Osan could fill your needs. My fellow pilots had thoroughly briefed me about the clothing before I left Beale. The man I needed to see in Osan was Mr. Oh. Mr. Oh sold only custom made clothing and had been doing so for over 20 years. I visited his shop about a week after arriving at Osan. Mr. Oh took my measurements and showed me his cloth samples. Within ten days he had produced for me the following: three three-piece suits, two ski outfits, a tuxedo, and a leather-flying jacket. All the garments were expertly tailored, and each coat had my name stitched, in cursive, on the inside pocket. Total cost for the entire wardrobe was $300.

I was also introduced to Korean food. I found it spicy but I ate it with caution. After Muff's warning about kimchi, I avoided it on days before I flew.

The Korean mission was different from the recon mission I was used to. We weren't over there to take pictures; we were there to listen. Instead of loading a camera in the nose, cylindrical pods approximately 20 feet long were loaded under the wings. The left pod was installed for balance only; it was empty. The right pod could be opened and loaded with electronic gear on its internal racks. A variety of electronic equipment could be loaded hence the name given to our mission, ELINT, which stood for electronic intelligence gathering. We never knew exactly what they were loading in the racks but it was our understanding that this equipment could monitor phone calls and even uplink these calls to a satellite, which would relay the information to the NSA. All of this occurred real time.

When we flew we stayed south of the border. The normal mission would last eight or nine hours, with a takeoff at either 7:00 a.m. or

243

7:00 p.m. Our flight pattern included eight waypoints, which were loaded into the Omega, the aircraft navigation system. The autopilot would fly the points in order, 1 through 8, and the resultant flight path looked like a figure eight.

I was a rookie in Korea but the other two pilots were very experienced. Each had been here two or three times. Dave Kantor was married with no children; Ken Stafford was single.

Dave was known as the "Corvette Man." The armed forces had a special deal with General Motors. This deal allowed overseas airmen to purchase new cars at a great discount, basically at cost. The purchaser would order the car while he was overseas and the car would be waiting for him when he returned to the states. Dave bought a new Corvette every year. When he got back to the states, he picked up his car and drove it home. He then sold his "old" Corvette for more than he paid for it. He always had a new car and he always made money on the deal. He was smart and lucky.

I was acting as mobile for Dave one day at Osan. Dave was doing the standard mission with the morning departure so there was not a lot of flight planning involved. I had pre-flighted his airplane earlier, and then joined him at the PSD building as he completed his pre-breathing. Once that was done, he climbed on the van for the ride out to the airplane. I followed along in the chase car. While Dave sat in the van, I rechecked the cockpit to ensure it was set up just the way he liked it.

Dave climbed out of the van and into the airplane. The techs connected him to the airplane's air conditioning and oxygen systems. When they finished, I hopped up beside the cockpit and gave all his connections one last look. He was ready so I gave him the thumbs up and he closed the canopy. The maintenance guys pulled the steps away and he started the engine. We followed him out to the end of the runway.

Security was very tight at Osan. The airplane was stored in a hangar when not flying. In order to get to the runway we had to taxi across a public road. The Security Police stopped traffic on both sides to allow the aircraft to taxi across. One of the vehicles waiting for Dave to taxi across the road was a workers' bus filled with early morning commuters coming on base. A security policeman noticed someone with a camera at one of the bus's windows. The policeman boarded the bus and took the film from every camera on the bus, whether it was used or not. Once the bus was film-free, Dave resumed his taxi to the runway.

When I acted as mobile, I always rolled down my window after the airplane had been cleared for takeoff. It was easier to see or hear if anything was amiss than if I was sitting in the car with the window full up. The weather that day was typical Osan winter weather. A solid cloud layer started at 1,000 feet and went up to about 12,000 feet. Dave's airplane looked good as he powered up and roared down the runway.

The U-2 on takeoff is an extremely loud airplane. Standing at the end of the runway for the takeoff was a bone-rattling experience. After the airplane rotated for takeoff, it climbed very quickly. Dave's airplane disappeared into the clouds in seconds. As I started to roll down the runway to retrieve the pogos, suddenly there was dead silence. I couldn't see his airplane but that sudden cutoff of noise meant only one thing. Dave's engine had quit.

I stared up at the clouds and saw his airplane break out the bottom of the cloud layer, still silent. He continued to descend but could not land. He was too high, his gear was up, and he was too fast. No sooner had I seen his airplane come out of the clouds I heard a tremendous roar. He had restarted the engine, and then, just as quickly as he had popped below the clouds, he pulled up and disappeared into them again. I ran to the radio to find out what the hell was going on. Dave told me that the engine quit as soon as he entered the clouds. He maintained his heading and pitched the nose over while hitting the start button. He broke out of the bottom and was reaching for the ejection seat handle when the engine restarted. He said it seemed to be running OK now so he elected to continue. He came back on schedule eight hours later.

If the engine had not restarted, Dave would have ejected. The U-2 ejection seat was state-of-the-art. The same seat was in the SR-71. It was a "0/0" seat. This meant that it would safely eject the pilot while sitting still on the ground - 0 speed and 0 altitude.

When Dave returned from this mission, the maintenance techs did a thorough inspection of the engine and found nothing amiss. It was just one of those things.

About a week later, it was Ken's turn to fly with Dave acting as his mobile. This time Ken had another engine problem but nothing like the one Dave had.

Ken had the morning departure and all looked good for his 7:00 a.m. launch. The weather was not only bad at Osan; the entire Korean peninsula was fogged in. Every U-2 mission had a thorough weather briefing. The pilot needed to know where to go if he couldn't land back at his origination station. That morning, his weather alternate was Kunsan Air Base, southwest of Osan. The ceiling and visibility at Kunsan were low but were adequate for a normal alternate.

Ken was two hours into his flight when he had a serious engine problem. This, coupled with weather conditions, made for an emergency situation. The J-75 engine in the U-2 was normally operated at a high Exhaust Gas Temperature (EGT). If the EGT was exceeded, a red warning light illuminated and the pilot would pull back on the throttle. You didn't want to leave the red light on because doing so risked an engine failure or fire. Ken saw the red light come on and throttled back slightly. This would normally bring the EGT down and extinguish the light. That day it didn't work; the light stayed on. So he reduced it a little more and the EGT came down, but then climbed right back up and turned on the light.

Ken reviewed his options. He had to get the airplane into position at an airport where he could make an engine out landing. He needed good weather for that and there was no good weather in Korea. In fact, the nearest place he could take the airplane was Okinawa, Japan; a distance of about 800 miles across the East China Sea. He informed all the appropriate agencies about his plans and he turned the airplane towards Japan. The engine would run for about 20 minutes before it started to overtemp. He would pull the throttle to idle and, in order to stay on speed, start descending. He then pushed the power up, started climbing, and watched the EGT climb. When the red light came on, it was back to idle and another descent. He did this vertical zigzag all the way to Okinawa. When he finally reached Okinawa the EGT climbed into the red even in idle power. Ken set himself up for an engine out approach and landing and then shut down his engine. He made an uneventful engine out landing and for his effort, didn't have to buy a drink at the Officers Club that night.

The U-2 maintenance team found a faulty fuel control valve in the engine. Once it was replaced, the engine ran great and Ken flew the airplane back to Osan.

It only seems fair that I have my own horror story to relate. It was, after all, my turn.

I was scheduled for the evening monitor mission with the normal 7:00 p.m. departure time. I was expected to land around 4:00 a.m. My figure-

8 track was just south of the demilitarized zone (DMZ) separating North and South Korea. I had flown this night mission a couple of times already and still had trouble with my body clock. I tried but couldn't force myself to sleep during the day prior to flight. I even tried pills given to me by the Flight Surgeon, but nothing seemed to work. I was able to get around two hours of sleep prior to flight. I felt OK when I started but that would change.

Dave was acting as mobile and he did his usual thorough job of preflight. We discussed the weather. It was fine for launch but a cold front was moving in with a forecast of rain showers and even a few thunderstorms possible. Take off and departure were normal. All was going smoothly as I eased the airplane into its flight track.

It was a moonless night with a thickening cloud layer rolling in below me. One of the most wondrous experiences of flying the U-2 happens during night flights, especially moonless ones. The feeling I had was of being suspended in a star-filled room. The higher you go, the brighter the stars get. So being above 70,000 feet on a pitch black night was magical. There were stars everywhere: up, down, and on either side. It was a view that never disappointed, and one I will never forget. It was on nights such as these that I felt I had reached those stars that I viewed from our roof behind the hardware store so many years ago. I was finally doing what I had dreamed about.

I settled into orbit and did my best to stay awake. I wasn't sure, but I think I may have dozed off with my eyes open. I shook my head and looked around to make sure everything was where it was supposed to be, and it was. The sudden realization that I may have fallen asleep really got my heart pumping and now I was truly awake. Then I felt something, a slight, small shudder. I quickly checked the airspeed and saw that it had dropped dangerously close to stall speed. Just then, the speed started to rise, right up through normal target speed and kept on going. Then another shudder, this one more pronounced. The speed then started down again. The autopilot was very subtly pitching the airplane up and down trying to control the speed but it wasn't working.

With each cycle, the speed came closer to the stall speed. It would then overcorrect and push the Mach buffet on the other end. The U-2 autopilot was made for use above 50,000 feet. Below 50,000, it was useless. Conversely, trying to fly the airplane without using the autopilot above 50,000 feet was nearly impossible. In order to hand fly the airplane, you had to use the instruments: the attitude director indicator (ADI), the vertical velocity indicator, and the airspeed indicator all were used to keep the target speed in the safe range. The problem was, subtle changes had to be made on the ADI. This gauge was about four inches across and making the minutest change in pitch would result in large excursions in vertical velocity. I couldn't allow the autopilot to either stall or Mach-buffet the airplane so I disconnected it and started hand flying the airplane.

The concentration required to keep the speed in the target range was all consuming. I thought I had leveled the airplane. It looked level on the ADI, but checking the vertical velocity, I was descending at 1000 feet per minute and my speed was building. To counteract this, I made a minute pitch change on the ADI, but that caused me to start climbing at 1000 feet per minute and the speed was dropping toward stall speed. While I was doing this vertical yo-yo, I also had to navigate in order to remain on my figure-8 track. The smallest excursion to my track would put me into North Korea. I was starting to hyperventilate. I recognized this and took steps to slow down my breathing. Since I was now working so hard, I was sweating profusely.

I realized that this roller coaster ride could result in a stall or Mach buffet, either of which would tear the tail off the airplane. If I didn't stay on my assigned track, I might be bailing out over a very hostile country. Even if I stayed on track but had to bail out, the wind below 50,000 feet might carry my chute to the north. These thoughts rushed through my head as I struggled to control the airplane. All the missions we flew were vital to our security so I tried to stay on station as long as possible, but it wasn't meant to be. I headed back to Osan. The two-hour battle with the airplane had left me exhausted.

The weather at Osan was cloudy with imbedded rain showers. The wind was gusting but at least it wasn't a crosswind. One of the drawbacks of the airplane was lack of weather radar. This is not a problem if you're flying over a thunderstorm during the day. Coming in to land at night with thunderstorms around the airport was a problem. My strategy for getting through the storms was called avoidance. I would turn the airplane away from a lightning flash, which I did several times on my descent .By turning away from the flashes, I didn't enter a thunderstorm and I didn't get hit by lightning. It must have been my lucky night. I summoned what remained of my strength for the approach and landing. It was a windy, rainy, rough ride but I landed safely. I turned the airplane over to maintenance, went back to my Q, and slept for 14 hours.

I now had my own war story to pass along to any new guy willing to listen. The rest of my tour passed by quickly. My two months were up and I went home to Beale.

Chapter 11

When I got home, we took some vacation time. I rented one of those giant motor homes and we drove all the way down the Pacific Coast Highway to San Diego. We stopped along the way camping at several beaches. The kids really loved the San Diego Zoo and Sea World. By the end of the tenth day, although we had a good time, we were all ready to get out of this motor home and back to our real home.

One of the perks of being in the U-2 squadron (in addition to the orange flight suits) was the lack of additional duties. Every type of flying squadron in the Air Force had additional duties the pilots had to perform. While at Craig as a T-38 instructor, for example, I was also the Runway Supervisory Unit (RSU) scheduler. Other IPs were safety officers, flight schedulers, ground training coordinators etc. In the U-2 outfit, my job was to fly the U-2. I was fortunate to also be able to fly the T-38. All the additional duties were handled by non-flying officers and enlisted personnel. When I returned from Osan the only thing I had to do was fly and that made my life very enjoyable.

After finishing a T-38 chase ride on the SR-71, I was sitting in our squadron talking with our Operations Officer, Lt Col Drake, when an announcement was made on the PA asking all available pilots to come to the briefing room. No reason for the meeting was mentioned. I heard a similar announcement the prior year and that turned out to be a Gary Powers visit. There were about 12 of us in the room that day from both the U-2 and the SR-71 squadrons.

Two guys in suits and earpieces entered the room and quickly looked around. When they were assured that it was safe, they summoned in the guest speaker. He was a small man, 5'5"or so. He too wore a suit and had shoulder-length blond hair. He started speaking in English but with a thick Russian accent. He didn't mention his name until the end but we all knew who he was because we were so familiar with his story. Standing before us was Viktor Bochenko; the man who had stolen a Russian MIG-25 Foxbat two years earlier.

Bochenko was a pilot with the Soviet Air Defense Forces based in Chuguyevka, Primorsky Krai. This was located northeast of Vladivostok in western USSR. He not only told us how he stole the jet but why he did it.

Like many in Russia at the time, Bochenko hated his communist overlords. Instead of being the worker's paradise it was purported to be, the USSR was a paradise for the party leadership only. Doctors, engineers, pilots and other skilled professionals were treated like unskilled laborers. Low wages, poor housing, and few amenities were the normal way of life for the vast majority of the population. Galling to him, more than anything else, was the lack of freedom. He and his family lived in an apartment house on base. The building was prefabricated somewhere else and shipped to his base in two pieces. They slapped the two pieces together on a muddy plain. The two pieces of the prefab building didn't quite fit together leaving many gaps at the joints. The construction crew filled in these gaps with mud and newspapers.

He dreamed of escape for a long time but the state's control of information prevented him from acting. Pilots were not allowed to have maps. The government didn't want them to know their exact location fearing just what Bochenko had in mind.

Soviet planes flew using an entirely different philosophy than their American counterparts. Radar ground controllers were in charge of Russian fighters. Once cleared for takeoff, pilots were told when to turn, climb, descend, accelerate, and decelerate. In formation flying, the lead aircraft followed the ground controller's instructions and the wingmen stayed in position, following lead.

Bochenko wanted out but he had to know exactly where he was and where he should go. There were no maps on base but there was a library in a nearby town. He found the maps he needed in that small library. He learned the exact location of his air base and also where he had to go to safely escape.

He started planning immediately. He decided he was going to Japan and he had to ensure that no one followed him. Japan was the only real option he had. It was the nearest non-communist country but he had to make it across the Sea of Japan to get there.

Several factors had to line up for this to work. It had to be done when the weather was good. He needed to navigate visually and be able to see the airport when he got there. He reasoned that he had to be the last plane in a formation flight: #3 in a 3 ship, or #4 in a 4 ship. He needed to have enough fuel to make his destination plus a little extra for insurance. The closest airport with a runway that would accommodate his aircraft was Japan's Hakodate Airport.

At the time of his defection, the MIG-25 was the most advanced Soviet fighter and he knew if he brought such a prize to the West, he could use his defection to bargain for his asylum.

September 6, 1976, was the day all his requirements were met. The weather was good enough to see the point of land in Russia he would use as his departure point. Once he hit that point, all he had to do was hold his heading across the Sea of Japan and wait for land to come into view. He was scheduled to be #3 in a 3-ship formation. He coaxed his support crew into giving him some extra fuel. Now all he had to do was wait for the right time to execute his escape maneuver. The right time turned out to be an echelon turn. An echelon turn has number two and number three behind the lead. Bochenko could see lead and number two but they couldn't see him. As lead and two went into a left turn Bochenko rolled right, dropped his altitude down to the deck, and lit his afterburners. In short order he was down at 100 feet going in excess of Mach 1.5. He hit his spot on the coast, took up his heading, and waited for land to appear.

He felt confident that no one was following him. He throttled back because his fuel was disappearing rapidly due to use of the afterburners. His defection would be meaningless if he had to ditch at sea. He saw Japan in the distance but he stayed low until he was within a few miles of Hokodate airport. He lined up on initial at 2,000 feet but he was doing 400 knots. He had to slow down if he wanted to land. He didn't have enough fuel left to go around and try for a second approach. He slowed as best he could; configured the airplane with gear and flaps and started his final turn. He was still high and fast but he had to make this approach work. He slammed the aircraft down on the runway and stomped on the brakes. The twin drag chutes automatically deployed, but he was still too fast. He ran off the end of the runway and his airplane settled into the mud, but it was undamaged.

This was the first time western experts were able to get a close look at the MIG-25 and it revealed many secrets and surprises. One of the surprises was how crudely manufactured the aircraft was. All U.S. aircraft wings, for example, were flush riveted, giving the wing a continuous, smooth surface. The MIG's wings had rivets sticking up all across them. The U.S. was making Maseratis; the Russians were building flying tanks.

The Japanese initially only allowed the U.S. to do a cursory examination of the MIG. This included ground testing the radar and the engines.

Later, the Japanese relented and invited the Americans to examine the plane extensively; and it was dismantled for this purpose. When the Americans had finished their analysis of the airplane, the Japanese loaded it into 30 crates and placed them aboard a Russian cargo ship. The crates arrived back in Russia in November 1976.

As for Bochenko, President Ford granted him asylum and a trust fund was set up for him, giving him a very comfortable living in his later years. U.S. intelligence personnel interrogated him for five months and employed him as a consultant for several years thereafter. In 1980, the U.S. Congress enacted S2961, authorizing citizenship for Bochenko. President Carter signed it into law in October 1980.

Bochenko married a music teacher from North Dakota and had two children but later divorced. He never divorced his Russian wife he left behind but he did visit Moscow in 1995 on a business trip. It is not known if he saw his wife and son.

Chapter 12

There were fifteen pilots in our U-2 squadron. We all rotated to two or three overseas locations so the chances of meeting all the pilots while I was at Beale between rotations were remote. As pilots returned to Beale from overseas, I made a point of getting to know the ones new to me. One such returnee was Terry Reitman. I had heard accounts of U-2 bailouts from other squadron pilots. Terry had ejected and lived to tell about it. Once I got to know Terry, he filled in the details of his brush with death.

He launched from Alconbury Air Base, UK, in May 1975. Terry's mission was photo recon of the East and West German border. He was well above 70,000 feet when, without warning, the aircraft's control column pitched violently forward. Terry disconnected the autopilot and tried to pull the column back, but it wouldn't budge. The airplane pitched forward and started spinning out of control. Terry was able to transmit a "Mayday" message prior to ejection.

The ejection system had a high mode and a low mode. If you ejected at high altitude, like Terry did, the pilot and the seat (as one unit) were separated from the airplane. A drogue chute deployed stabilizing the pilot and his seat as they fell. A built-in altimeter in the seat assembly sent out a signal at 15,000 feet, activating a "butt snapper" separating the pilot from the seat. Once clear of the seat, the pilot's main chute deployed.

Terry was hanging from the chute descending and hoping that the prevailing winds would keep him in the west. The East Germans were on full alert having seen his plane on their radar prior to the ejection. Capturing a U-2 pilot in East German airspace would be a huge propaganda victory for the communists. The East Germans launched everything they had including fixed-wing aircraft and helicopters. Meanwhile, the USAF Search and Rescue team had been alerted along with the West Germans. Everyone was looking for Terry. The crippled aircraft had broken apart due to the high "G" forces but all the parts fell in West Germany. Terry landed in the West, in a heavily wooded area about 100 miles northeast of Bonn. He was uninjured.

What makes Terry's ejection story unusual is what happened to Jon Lister about a month before Terry's incident. Captain Jon Lister and Captain Jim Barron were ferrying two aircraft from U-Tapao, Thailand back to their home base (then Davis-Monthan AFB, Arizona). Their first stop was Guam, about an eight-hour flight. The aircraft departed about five minutes apart and both were climbing above 65,000 feet. A KC-135 tanker was escorting the two ferries. The tanker was carrying the two relief pilots who would take over in Guam for Lister and Barron. Also aboard the tanker were maintenance personnel, spare parts and supplies.

An hour and thirty minutes into the flight, the control column in Lister's airplane slammed forward causing the plane to porpoise (go up and down). Lister disengaged the autopilot, pulled back on the throttle, and tried to pull the control column back. It wouldn't budge. The airplane pitched over and started spinning out of control. Lister was able to make one radio transmission, "out of control, upside down, and spinning," he said. The last thing he remembered was reaching for the eject handle. As he left the airplane, something hit him in the forehead, cracking the face shield of his helmet and knocking him unconscious.

Lister fell more than 50,000 feet at a speed of over 600 miles per hour. For reasons unknown, the drogue chute, which was supposed to slow and stabilize him down to 15,000, did not deploy. He was in a free-fall more than three minutes before his main chute opened at 15,000 feet. He came down, still unconscious, in the Gulf of Siam. He was fortunate to be wearing a self-inflating life preserver. Without it, he probably would have drowned that night before regaining consciousness. When he did come to, he climbed into his raft. After Lister ejected, immediate search and rescue was initiated. A fisherman about 30 miles east of Pattani, a village north of the Malaysian border, picked him up. He was drifting in the Gulf for eight hours before being rescued.

That afternoon, a rescue helicopter arrived and took him back to his old base at Nakhon Phanom. From there he took a C-130 to U-Tapao where his support crew gave him a hero's welcome. Once back in the states, Lister was transferred, against his wishes, out of the U-2 squadron; even though the problem was in the airplane, not the pilot. He stayed in the Air Force until the end. He died of cancer in May 1987 and was buried on Memorial Day at his alma mater, West Point.

Chapter 13

One of the several U-2 pilots who had attended my solo party in 1977 was Dave Harrison. Dave did me the honor of dropping the U-2 pin into the yard of beer. Dave was an USAF Academy graduate and a very experienced pilot. He had been to every overseas location more than once. Dave was married to a beautiful woman and had two great kids. He deployed to Akrotiri Royal Air Base in Cyprus in November 1977. On December 7, 1977, Dave took off, fully fueled, for a photo recon mission over the Sinai. He attempted a tight turn after takeoff but it turned out to be too tight. As the airplane rolled into the turn, Dave realized he had too much bank so he tried to roll out. Due to the steep bank angle, his ailerons had stalled. The airplane would not respond to his inputs and roll out; the bank angle only increased. Dave stayed with the airplane hoping he could save it but he was doomed. The airplane crashed into a radar shack on the side of the runway killing Dave along with the senior meteorological officer and four locally employed assistants.

Dave was on my mind when I received my assignment to Cyprus in December 1978, one year after his accident. I read the accident report but found it hard to believe that this highly intelligent and experienced pilot could get himself into an unrecoverable position. The aileron stall he experienced was something I had never heard about before his accident. Other U-2 pilots were all unfamiliar with it, too. But we all learned from it and sharp turns after takeoff stopped after Dave's accident.

I was touring the runway facilities at Akrotiri soon after my arrival. The crash site was still plainly visible. The site was littered with baseball-sized rocks. I poked around in these rocks and saw something. I had found a piece of Dave's airplane about three inches square. I still have that piece and keep it as a reminder to fly within the limits, both my own and those of the airplane. There's an old aviation saying that I have lived by in my aviation career: "There are old pilots, and there are bold pilots; but there are no old, bold pilots."

I had been looking forward to this Cyprus rotation since I joined the squadron. Everything about this place was beautiful - the weather, the food, and the flying. Cyprus is a beautiful green gem set in the blue Mediterranean. It is officially known as the Republic of Cyprus and is the third largest and third most populous island in the Mediterranean. Earliest human activity on the island can be traced to the 10th millennium B.C.. Greek culture dominated the island after its conquest by Alexander the Great in 333 B.C. The island was placed under British administration in 1878, and eventually gained its independence in 1960. The British, however, retained control of two areas of the island, Akrotiri and Dhekelia. These two areas were known as sovereign base areas.

In 1974, violence between Greek and Turkish Cypriots prompted a Turkish invasion, resulting in a partition of the island. The Turks took over the north and the Greeks, the south. RAF Akrotiri is located on the southernmost tip of the island, just south of the city of Limassol.

The U-2 presence on the base was well known but unacknowledged by all. We did not wear our uniforms on base, strictly civilian clothes for us. Since we were westerners without a British accent, people knew immediately what we were doing there. We had one airplane, three pilots, and an operations officer. When the airplane wasn't flying it remained in a hangar out of the public view.

Our mission was photo reconnaissance. We rarely had a cancellation because of the great weather. Our job seemed simple. All the nations involved in the Middle East conflict, Egypt, Israel, Jordan, Lebanon, and Syria had agreed to allow U-2 overflights in order to verify that no one nation was cheating on the peace agreement. Our flights would verify, for example, that Egypt wasn't moving tanks across the Sinai, or that Israel wasn't placing artillery pieces into the Golan Heights. Satellites also kept an eye on things but satellite schedules could become known. Our missions were top secret and randomly scheduled. No one ever knew when we were coming.

Our typical track took us south out of Akrotiri, all the way across the Sinai, then northeast along the Jordan-Israel border. We then crossed over Syria, Lebanon, and back around to

Cyprus. The flight took about two hours, but it was seldom boring. It seemed that every time I flew this mission, a different group tried to shoot me down. One time the Egyptian Air Force scrambled interceptors after me; they didn't get close. Then it was the Israelis turn. They scrambled U.S. made F-15s after me. They didn't reach me either, but they got closer than the Egyptians. My highest pucker factor occurred thanks to the Syrians. The Syrians didn't launch aircraft to intercept me but they did track me with SAM missiles. They never did fire a missile but they did have my full attention. Keep in mind, all these countries knew who we were and why we were there and all had agreed to let us overfly them.

While the flying weather in Cyprus was unbeatable, our non-flying activities were just as good. The Brits had an active social calendar of parties and dinners. They treated us like family and we all got along wonderfully as long as we didn't talk about work. Our social philosophy was a variation on the Russian peasants' lament about their communist overlords: "They pretend to pay us and we pretend to work." Ours was: " We pretended not to be there and they pretended not to see us."

When I wasn't flying or acting as mobile, I spent my time exploring the island (only the Greek side). Looking back after years of travel, I still feel it was the most beautiful place I'd ever seen. I spent days exploring the Roman ruins on the island. One scene I recall with clarity is sitting in a Roman amphitheater, perched above the beautiful blue sea as I watched the setting sun. I roamed through the streets of Paphos and visited the rock where Aphrodite appeared from the foam of the sea. It was a truly magical place.

No description of Cyprus is complete without discussing its food. All the food was fresh, local, delicious and very healthy. The lamb dishes were simple but exquisite. The local fruits and vegetables sold at the small farmer's stands just off base made healthy eating a pleasure. At the time we didn't even think about the obvious health benefits of eating fresh, local produce, or salads drizzled with olive oil produced from trees right down the road from us. We just ate it because it was delicious.

The two and one half months on the island raced by. It was one of the few places where I wanted to remain rather than go home. My time in paradise had come to an end, however, and it was back to the real world.

Chapter 14

When I had completed my medical evaluation at Brooks Army Medical Center in 1977, I was told that if I wanted to continue flying, I would have to return every two years to Brooks and repeat the entire process. I'd have to do this in spite of having a clean bill of health. As long as that initial doctor's assessment of coronary artery disease was in my record, I had to go back there if I wanted to continue flying.

My supervisors at Beale encouraged me to seek a position at Strategic Air Command's headquarters at Offut AFB, Nebraska. They advised me that for my own "career progression," I needed to move to a staff position, a non-flying job. The logic of their argument escaped me. All of the time, training, and experience required to get me into the U-2 would be wasted. The Air Force believed in career advancement achieved through broadening your experience by holding command positions. If a pilot wished to remain flying, his career advancement was dead. USAF was willing to invest countless dollars into a pilot's training only to remove him from the cockpit and place him behind a desk. One of the problems with the military was, and still is, that it was not cost effective. Money was meaningless. A good example of this is the yearly budget. If an individual Wing didn't spend as much as the previous year, their budget would be cut the following year. As the fiscal year came to a close, outfits would schedule additional flights to ensure that they didn't come up short.

This happened to me in the C-130 while on rotation in Europe. We weren't scheduled to fly but ops told us to take an airplane and put 15 hours on it in the next three days. This was done to bring our spending up to the level of the previous year. So we went off to Rota Spain, Athens, and Aviano Italy.

When I returned to Beale in February 1979, these two issues - the medical re-evaluation, and the push to move to a desk job - dominated my thinking. I had the best flying job in the world but in order to continue flying I had to consider something duller but better paying - an airline job.

I wasn't the only one faced with this dilemma. Seven of my fellow U-2 pilots put in their separation papers. The airlines in the spring of 1979 had started hiring again. They had cut back over the past ten years but now the hiring boom was in full swing. I interviewed with several airlines and chose Eastern Airlines.

After leaving the Air Force we headed back to Philadelphia to see family and friends. I visited with my mom and we discussed the decision to separate from the service. I told her that it was a painful decision and that I would miss the exciting life I had for the past ten years. She helped me put it all into perspective by recalling our time together in that small apartment behind the hardware store in Germantown. She talked about those nights on the roof and how I told her that I wanted to reach the stars. She reminded me that I was able to follow my dream and achieve the goal I had set so many years ago. I realized she was right.

I considered the Air Force a flying fraternity, a family to me. I'll always treasure the memories of the people I met in the service. We dedicated ourselves to this great nation and I believe that we did our part to keep freedom alive.

P.S. My mom died peacefully on Thanksgiving Day, 2014.

Printed in Poland
by Amazon Fulfillment
Poland Sp. z o.o., Wrocław